CSET Mathematics Study Gu
Subtest I: Algebra; Number Theory

Copyright 2009 by Christopher Goff

University of the Pacific

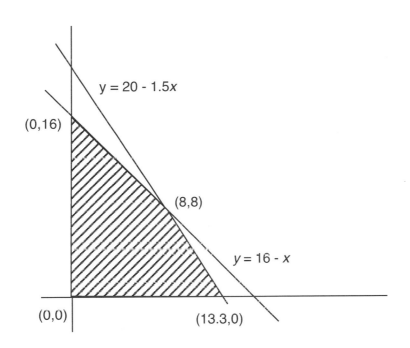

CSET Topic Domains Covered:

1.1 Algebraic Structures

a. Know why the real and complex numbers are each a field, and that particular rings are not fields (e.g., integers, polynomial rings, matrix rings)

1. What is a field? What are some examples?

   A field is a set F together with two operations (called $+$ and $\times$) satisfying the following properties. Suppose that a, b, and c are elements of F.

   (a) F is closed under $+$ and $\times$

   This means that $a + b$ and $a \times b$, also called ab, are elements of F. [The element $a \times b$ is often written ab. We will follow this conventional notation below.]

   (b) $+$ and $\times$ are associative

   This means that $(a + b) + c = a + (b + c)$ and $(ab)c = a(bc)$.

   (c) $+$ and $\times$ are commutative

   This means that $a + b = b + a$ and $ab = ba$.

   (d) $+$ and $\times$ have identity elements 0 and 1 in F, respectively

   This means that $a + 0 = a$ and $b \cdot 1 = b$.

   (e) every element has an additive inverse in F

   This means that for every a in F, there is an element $-a$ **in** F satisfying $a + (-a) = 0$.

   (f) every non-zero element has a multiplicative inverse in F

   If $b \neq 0$, then there is $\frac{1}{b}$ **in** F satisfying $b(\frac{1}{b}) = 1$.

   (g) $\times$ distributes over $+$

   This means that $a(b + c) = ab + ac$.

   The most common fields we use are the rational numbers, the real numbers, and the complex numbers.

2. What is a ring? What are some examples?

   A ring is a set R together with two operations (called $+$ and $\times$) satisfying the following properties.

   (a) R is closed under $+$ and $\times$

   (b) $+$ and $\times$ are associative

   (c) $+$ is commutative

   (d) $+$ and $\times$ have identity elements 0 and 1 in R, respectively

   (e) every element has an additive inverse in R

   (f) $\times$ distributes over $+$

There are two key differences between the definition of a ring and the definition of a field: (1) rings do not necessarily have a commutative multiplication, and (2) rings do not necessarily contain multiplicative inverses. Notice that every field is a ring, but that there are rings which are not fields.

The most common rings we use (in addition to the fields listed above) are the integers, the set of square matrices of a given size (like all 2 by 2 matrices, for instance), and the set of polynomials with coefficients in another ring.

3. What are some non-examples of fields and rings?

The following common rings are not fields: integers, the set of square matrices of a given size (like all 2 by 2 matrices, for instance), and the set of polynomials with coefficients in another ring.

The natural numbers are not a ring. The set of all quadratic polynomials is not a ring. See Sample Problems, below.

4. Sample Problems

   (a) Give an example of a ring that is not a field.

   (b) Why are the integers not a field?

   (c) Why are the natural numbers not a ring?

   (d) Why is the set of all quadratic polynomials not a ring?

   (e) Write the multiplicative inverse of $3 - 2i$ in $a + bi$ form.

   (f) Show that the set of 2 by 2 matrices with integer entries forms a non-commutative ring.

   (g) Prove that the set of 2 by 2 invertible matrices with complex number entries is NOT a field.

   (h) Write the multiplicative inverse of $x + yi$ in $a + bi$ form.

   (i) What is the smallest field that contains 0 and 1?

   (j) Using the field properties listed above, prove that $(a + b)c = ac + bc$.

   (k) Let F be the field of rational functions $\dfrac{p(x)}{q(x)}$, where $p(x)$ and $q(x)$ are any polynomials with real coefficients and $q(x) \neq 0$.

      i. Show that F contains a multiplicative identity element.

     ii. Show that F is closed under multiplication.

    iii. Show that F is closed under addition.

    iv. Show that every non-zero element of F is invertible.

5. Answers to Sample Problems

   (a) Give an example of a ring that is not a field. Examples include: the integers, polynomials, and the set of all square matrices of a given size.

(b) Why are the integers not a field? Because not every integer has a multiplicative inverse *that is an integer*. For instance, the multiplicative inverse of 3 is $\frac{1}{3}$, which is not an integer.

(c) Why are the natural numbers not a ring? Because they do not contain an additive identity (although you might see a textbook which includes 0 in the natural numbers). Also, the additive inverses of natural numbers are not natural numbers. For instance, the additive inverse of 3 is -3, which is not a natural number.

(d) Why is the set of all quadratic polynomials not a ring? The set of quadratic polynomials is not closed under multiplication. For instance, if you multiply $x^2 + 1$ by $x^2 - 1$, you obtain $x^4 - 1$, which is not quadratic.

(e) Write the multiplicative inverse of $3 - 2i$ in $a + bi$ form.

$$\frac{1}{3 - 2i} \cdot \frac{3 + 2i}{3 + 2i} = \frac{3 + 2i}{9 - 4i^2} = \frac{3 + 2i}{9 + 4} = \frac{3}{13} + \frac{2}{13}i.$$

(f) Show that the set of 2 by 2 matrices with integer entries forms a non-commutative ring. We will show a few of the properties directly and leave the rest to the reader. To see the closure under addition, we technically should show that the sum

$$\begin{bmatrix} a & b \\ c & d \end{bmatrix} + \begin{bmatrix} a' & b' \\ c' & d' \end{bmatrix} = \begin{bmatrix} a + a' & b + b' \\ c + c' & d + d' \end{bmatrix}$$

is again a two by two matrix of integers. But since the integers are closed under addition, each entry of the new matrix is an integer. Hence the set of 2 by 2 matrices of integers is closed under addition. We will show multiplication as well (in part to remind the reader about how to multiply matrices).

$$\begin{bmatrix} a & b \\ c & d \end{bmatrix} \cdot \begin{bmatrix} a' & b' \\ c' & d' \end{bmatrix} = \begin{bmatrix} aa' + bc' & ab' + bd' \\ ca' + dc' & cb' + dd' \end{bmatrix}$$

Since the set of integers is closed under multiplication and addition, each entry in the product matrix is again an integer. Hence the set of 2 by 2 matrices with integer entries is closed under matrix multiplication.

We now check that matrix addition is commutative. Since

$$\begin{bmatrix} a & b \\ c & d \end{bmatrix} + \begin{bmatrix} a' & b' \\ c' & d' \end{bmatrix} = \begin{bmatrix} a + a' & b + b' \\ c + c' & d + d' \end{bmatrix} = \begin{bmatrix} a' & b' \\ c' & d' \end{bmatrix} + \begin{bmatrix} a & b \\ c & d \end{bmatrix},$$

it certainly follows that matrix addition is commutative.

Most of the other properties involve straightforward checks, under two conditions. First, the additive identity element of this ring is the *zero matrix*, $\begin{bmatrix} 0 & 0 \\ 0 & 0 \end{bmatrix}$, while the multiplicative identity element is the *identity matrix*, $\begin{bmatrix} 1 & 0 \\ 0 & 1 \end{bmatrix}$.

To show that this ring is not commutative, we need to give an example of two matrices that do not commute:

$$\begin{bmatrix} 0 & 1 \\ 0 & 0 \end{bmatrix} \cdot \begin{bmatrix} 0 & 0 \\ 1 & 0 \end{bmatrix} = \begin{bmatrix} 1 & 0 \\ 0 & 0 \end{bmatrix},$$

whereas

$$\begin{bmatrix} 0 & 0 \\ 1 & 0 \end{bmatrix} \cdot \begin{bmatrix} 0 & 1 \\ 0 & 0 \end{bmatrix} = \begin{bmatrix} 0 & 0 \\ 0 & 1 \end{bmatrix}$$

Since these answers are different, then certainly the two matrices $\begin{bmatrix} 0 & 1 \\ 0 & 0 \end{bmatrix}$ and $\begin{bmatrix} 0 & 0 \\ 1 & 0 \end{bmatrix}$ do not commute. Hence the ring of 2 by 2 matrices with integer entries is NOT commutative.

(g) Prove that the set of 2 by 2 invertible matrices with complex number entries is NOT a field. We will show that this set of matrices is not closed under addition. Recall that $1 = 1 + 0i$ is a complex number. We have

$$\begin{bmatrix} 1 & 0 \\ 0 & 1 \end{bmatrix} + \begin{bmatrix} -1 & 0 \\ 0 & -1 \end{bmatrix} = \begin{bmatrix} 0 & 0 \\ 0 & 0 \end{bmatrix},$$

which is clearly not an invertible matrix, even though each matrix summand is invertible. Another reason is that the additive identity, the zero matrix, is not invertible and is therefore not an element of the set of 2 by 2 invertible matrices with complex number entries. Hence the set of 2 by 2 invertible matrices with complex number entries is not a field.

(h) Write the multiplicative inverse of $x + yi$ in $a + bi$ form.

$$\frac{1}{x+yi} \cdot \frac{x-yi}{x-yi} = \frac{x-yi}{x^2 - i^2 y^2} = \frac{x-yi}{x^2 + y^2} = \frac{x}{x^2 + y^2} - \frac{y}{x^2 + y^2}i.$$

(i) What is the smallest field that contains 0 and 1? Since any field must be closed under addition and must contain additive inverses, we know that all positive and negative integers must lie in this field. Moreover, since fields must contain multiplicative inverses of all nonzero elements, we must have the numbers $\frac{1}{2}$, $\frac{1}{3}$, etc. in the field. Then, using closure under addition and multiplication, we can obtain any rational number. It turns out that the rational numbers form a field. Thus, the rational numbers are the smallest field containing zero and one (under usual operations). [If you want to use operations mod 2 $(1+1 = 0)$, then you can make a field containing only 0 and 1!]

(j) Using the field properties listed above, prove that $(a + b)c = ac + bc$. We have $(a + b)c = c(a + b) = ca + cb = ac + bc$, where we have used the commutativity of multiplication and the distributive property in the way it was originally stated above.

(k) Let F be the field of rational functions $\dfrac{p(x)}{q(x)}$, where $p(x)$ and $q(x)$ are any polynomials with real coefficients and $q(x) \neq 0$.

   i. Show that F contains a multiplicative identity element. The element $1 = \frac{1}{1}$ is an element of F, because 1 is a (degree zero) polynomial.

   ii. Show that F is closed under multiplication.

$$\frac{p(x)}{q(x)} \cdot \frac{a(x)}{b(x)} = \frac{p(x)a(x)}{q(x)b(x)}$$

Polynomials are closed under multiplication. Since $q(x)$ and $b(x)$ are not 0, then $q(x)b(x) \neq 0$. So the product of two elements of F is another element of F.

iii. Show that F is closed under addition.

$$\frac{p(x)}{q(x)} + \frac{a(x)}{b(x)} = \frac{p(x)b(x) + q(x)a(x)}{q(x)b(x)}$$

Again, since polynomials are closed under multiplication and addition, and since the denominator is not zero, the sum of two elements of F is again an element of F.

iv. Show that every non-zero element of F is invertible. If $\frac{p(x)}{q(x)} \neq 0$, then $p(x) \neq 0$. So that means that $\frac{q(x)}{p(x)}$ is an element of F. Multiplying, we get

$$\frac{p(x)}{q(x)} \cdot \frac{q(x)}{p(x)} = \frac{p(x)q(x)}{p(x)q(x)} = 1.$$

Hence, every non-zero element of F is invertible.

b. Apply basic properties of real and complex numbers in constructing mathematical arguments (e.g., if $a < b$ and $c < 0$, then $ac > bc$)

1. What are some basic properties of real and complex numbers?

   The field properties are the most basic properties of real and complex numbers. In addition, for the real numbers there are properties of ordering, like the Trichotomy Axiom (mentioned below), and the following. Fill in the blanks.

   (a) If $a < b$ and $c < d$, then $a + c$_____$b + d$.

   (b) If $a < b$ and $c > 0$, then ac_____bc.

   (c) If $a < b$ and $c < 0$, then ac_____bc.

   (d) If $a \leq b$ and $b \leq a$, then a_____b.

   (e) If $a < b$ and $b < c$, then a_____c.

   (f) (Trichotomy) If a and b are real numbers, then exactly one of the following is true: $a < b$, $a > b$, or a_____b.

   ANS: $<$, $<$, $>$, $=$, $<$, $=$.

   There are also properties of equality. List as many as you can:

   ANS: Reflexive, Symmetric, and Transitive Properties of Equality, Additive Property of Equality, Multiplicative Property of Equality

2. What is the definition of a rational number? ...of a complex number?

   A rational number can be expressed as the ratio of two integers. So, any rational number can be written as $\frac{p}{q}$, where p and q are integers, and $q \neq 0$.

A complex number can be expressed as the sum of a real number and an imaginary number. So, any complex number can be written as $a+bi$, where a and b are real numbers and $i^2 = -1$. What is an imaginary number?

ANS: An imaginary number is one satisfying $x^2 \leq 0$. [There is sometimes a debate on whether 0 is imaginary or not. I choose to think of 0 as $0i$ in this case, making it imaginary. It's also real. No one said that numbers had to be either real or imaginary, but not both.]

3. Sample Problems

   (a) Explain why the solution to $3x - 5 = 4$ is $x = 3$ by showing each step. List all the properties you use.

   (b) Explain why the solution to $-3x - 5 < 4$ is $x > -3$ by showing each step. List all the properties you use.

   (c) What is proved by the following?

   Suppose that $\sqrt{2} = \frac{p}{q}$, where $\frac{p}{q}$ is written in lowest terms; i.e., p and q are integers that have no common factors other than 1. Then $2 = \frac{p^2}{q^2}$. Since p and q have no common factors, we must have $q = 1$ or else $\frac{p^2}{q^2}$ would not be an integer. So $q = 1$ and $p^2 = 2$. But this is impossible because there is no integer p with $p^2 = 2$. $\square$

   (d) Show on a number line that if $a > b > 0$, then $-a < -b$.

   (e) Let a and b be integers with $b \neq 0$. Consider the following statement: If $\frac{a}{b} < 1$, then $a < b$.

      i. List some values for a and b that make the statement true.
      ii. List some values for a and b that make the statement false.
      iii. What is a condition on a and/or b that will make the statement necessarily true?

   (f) Using various ring properties and properties of equality, give reasons for the proof of the Multiplication Property of Zero: If x is in a ring, then $0x = 0$.

      - $0 + 0 = 0$
      - $(0 + 0)x = 0x$
      - $0x + 0x = 0x$
      - $0x + 0x = 0x + 0$
      - $0x = 0$.

4. Answers to Sample Problems

   (a) Explain why the solution to $3x - 5 = 4$ is $x = 3$ by showing each step. List all the properties you use.

$$3x - 5 = 4 \qquad \text{Given}$$
$$(3x - 5) + 5 = 4 + 5 \qquad \text{Additive Property of Equality}$$
$$(3x - 5) + 5 = 9 \qquad \text{Arithmetic}$$
$$(3x + (-5)) + 5 = 9 \qquad \text{Definition of Subtraction}$$
$$3x + ((-5) + 5) = 9 \qquad \text{Associative Property of Addition}$$
$$3x + 0 = 9 \qquad \text{Additive Inverse}$$
$$3x = 9 \qquad \text{Additive Identity}$$
$$\frac{1}{3}(3x) = \frac{1}{3}(9) \qquad \text{Multiplicative Property of Equality}$$
$$\frac{1}{3}(3x) = 3 \qquad \text{Arithmetic}$$
$$\left(\frac{1}{3} \cdot 3\right)x = 3 \qquad \text{Associative Property of Multiplication}$$
$$1x = 3 \qquad \text{Multiplicative Inverse}$$
$$x = 3 \qquad \text{Multiplicative Identity}$$

(b) Explain why the solution to $-3x - 5 < 4$ is $x > -3$ by showing each step. List all the properties you use.

$$-3x - 5 < 4 \qquad \text{Given}$$
$$(-3x - 5) + 5 < 4 + 5 \qquad \text{Additive Property of Inequality}$$
$$(-3x - 5) + 5 < 9 \qquad \text{Arithmetic}$$
$$(-3x + (-5)) + 5 < 9 \qquad \text{Definition of Subtraction}$$
$$-3x + ((-5) + 5) < 9 \qquad \text{Associative Property of Addition}$$
$$-3x + 0 < 9 \qquad \text{Additive Inverse}$$
$$-3x < 9 \qquad \text{Additive Identity}$$
$$-\frac{1}{3}(-3x) > -\frac{1}{3}(9) \qquad \text{Multiplicative Property of Inequality}$$
$$-\frac{1}{3}(-3x) > -3 \qquad \text{Arithmetic}$$
$$\left(-\frac{1}{3} \cdot -3\right)x > -3 \qquad \text{Associative Property of Multiplication}$$
$$1x > -3 \qquad \text{Multiplicative Inverse}$$
$$x > -3 \qquad \text{Multiplicative Identity}$$

(c) What is proved by the following?

Suppose that $\sqrt{2} = \frac{p}{q}$, where $\frac{p}{q}$ is written in lowest terms; i.e., p and q are integers that have no common factors other than 1. Then $2 = \frac{p^2}{q^2}$. Since p and q have no common factors, we must have $q = 1$ or else $\frac{p^2}{q^2}$ would not be an integer. So $q = 1$ and $p^2 = 2$. But this is impossible because there is no integer p with $p^2 = 2$. $\square$

This is a proof (by contradiction) that $\sqrt{2}$ is irrational. The proof started by assuming that $\sqrt{2}$ was rational and deduced a contradiction to that assumption. Hence $\sqrt{2}$ must be irrational.

(d) Show on a number line that if $a > b > 0$, then $-a < -b$. We are told that $a > b > 0$. On a number line, this looks like:

So, if we put in $-a$ and $-b$ as well, we get:

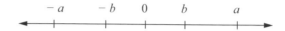

Clearly, $-a$ is to the left of $-b$, and thus $-a < -b$.

(e) Let a and b be integers with $b \neq 0$. Consider the following statement: If $\frac{a}{b} < 1$, then $a < b$.

   i. List some values for a and b that make the statement true. Answers may vary, although b must be greater than zero.

   ii. List some values for a and b that make the statement false. Answers may vary, although b must be less than zero.

   iii. What is a condition on a and/or b that will make the statement necessarily true? If b is positive, then one can use the Multiplicative Property of Inequality to deduce that the statement must be true. Conversely, if $b < 0$, then the statement is false.

(f) Using various ring properties and properties of equality, give reasons for the proof of the Multiplication Property of Zero: If x is in a ring, then $0x = 0$.

- $0 + 0 = 0$ Additive Identity (anything plus 0 equals itself)
- $(0 + 0)x = 0x$ Multiplicative Property of Equality
- $0x + 0x = 0x$ Distributive Property
- $0x + 0x = 0x + 0$ Additive Identity
- $0x = 0$.   Additive Property of Equality (in reverse)

c. Know that the rational numbers and real numbers can be ordered and that the complex numbers cannot be ordered, but that any polynomial equation with real coefficients can be solved in the complex field

1. What does it mean to be "ordered?"

   A set is "totally ordered" (or just "ordered") if, given any two elements a and b in the set, either $a \leq b$ or $b \leq a$. Notice that because of the Trichotomy Axiom of real numbers, we know that if x and y are real numbers, either (i) $x < y$, (ii) $x > y$, or (iii) $x = y$. Thus, the real numbers, and any subset of the real numbers, is ordered.

2. Why can't the complex numbers be ordered?

   This question is misleading. The complex numbers can indeed be ordered, but not in a meaningful way. We will examine some of the consequences of trying to order the complex numbers in the sample problems.

3. Fundamental Theorem of Algebra

We see in **1.2 Polynomial Equations and Inequalities** that the Fundamental Theorem of Algebra comes up. The Fundamental Theorem of Algebra says that if $f(x)$ is a polynomial with real coefficients, then $f(x)$ can be factored into linear and quadratic factors, each of which has real coefficients. Moreover, $f(x)$ can be factored entirely into linear factors if you allow your factors to have complex coefficients.

[Mathematicians say: Every complex polynomial has a root in $\mathbb{C}$. A fancy way to say this is to say that $\mathbb{C}$ is an "algebraically closed" field.]

4. Sample Problems

   (a) Which of the following sets is an ordered field: complex numbers, rational numbers, integers, or natural numbers?

   (b) List three reasons why the set of 2 by 2 matrices with real number entries do not form an ordered field.

   (c) What is the maximum number of complex solutions to $x^{17} - 573x^9 + 54x^8 - 167x + 2 = 0$?

   (d) One way to order the complex numbers is as follows: $(a + bi) \lll (c + di)$ if (1) $a < c$ or (2) $a = c$ and $b < d$. In other words, compare the real parts to determine which is bigger. If they are the same, then move to the imaginary parts.

      i. Which is bigger, 2 or 20?
      ii. Which is bigger, $1 + 2i$ or $1 + 20i$?
      iii. Which is bigger, $2 + i$ or $-100 - 100i$?
      iv. Which is bigger, $100i$ or 1?
      v. What might be a disadvantage to this ordering?

   (e) Another way to order the complex numbers is by their magnitudes. The magnitude of $a + bi$ is $\sqrt{a^2 + b^2}$, which is a real number. So, $(a + bi) \lll (c + di)$ if $\sqrt{a^2 + b^2} < \sqrt{c^2 + d^2}$.

      i. Which is bigger, 2 or 20?
      ii. Which is bigger, -2 or -20?
      iii. Which is bigger, 5 or $3 + 4i$?
      iv. Which is bigger, $1 + i$ or $1 - i$?
      v. What might be a disadvantage to this ordering?

5. Answers to Sample Problems

   (a) Which of the following sets is an ordered field: complex numbers, rational numbers, integers, or natural numbers? The rational numbers, integers, and natural numbers are all ordered via $<$, because they are subsets of the (ordered) real numbers.

   (b) List three reasons why the set of 2 by 2 matrices with real number entries do not form an ordered field. It's certainly hard to order them (in a meaningful way), but the set of 2 by 2 real matrices do not even form a field. Indeed, matrices like $\begin{bmatrix} 1 & 0 \\ 0 & 0 \end{bmatrix}$ do not even have a multiplicative inverse.

(c) What is the maximum number of complex solutions to $x^{17} - 573x^9 + 54x^8 - 167x + 2 = 0$? Seventeen. The only time there may be fewer than 17 complex roots is if some of the roots have a multiplicity greater than one (like double roots, triple roots, etc.).

(d) One way to order the complex numbers is as follows: $(a + bi) \lll (c + di)$ if (1) $a < c$ or (2) $a = c$ and $b < d$. In other words, compare the real parts to determine which is bigger. If they are the same, then move to the imaginary parts.

    i. Which is bigger, 2 or 20? ANS: 20

    ii. Which is bigger, $1 + 2i$ or $1 + 20i$? ANS: $1 + 20i$

    iii. Which is bigger, $2 + i$ or $-100 - 100i$? ANS: $2 + i$

    iv. Which is bigger, $100i$ or 1? ANS: 1

    v. What might be a disadvantage to this ordering? One disadvantage is that complex numbers with large imaginary parts but small real parts might be considered smaller than numbers that have small imaginary parts and only slightly bigger real parts. This method seems to give undue importance to the real part of a complex number.

(e) Another way to order the complex numbers is by their magnitudes. The magnitude of $a + bi$ is $\sqrt{a^2 + b^2}$, which is a real number. So, $(a + bi) \lll (c + di)$ if $\sqrt{a^2 + b^2} < \sqrt{c^2 + d^2}$.

    i. Which is bigger, 2 or 20? ANS: 20

    ii. Which is bigger, -2 or -20? ANS: -20

    iii. Which is bigger, 5 or $3 + 4i$? ANS: same magnitude

    iv. Which is bigger, $1 + i$ or $1 - i$? ANS: same magnitude

    v. What might be a disadvantage to this ordering? One disadvantage is that it is not consistent with the ordering of real numbers. ($-20 > -2$, for instance.) Another disadvantage is that sometimes very different-looking complex numbers have the same magnitude.

1.2 Polynomial Equations and Inequalities

a. Know why graphs of linear inequalities are half planes and be able to apply this fact (e.g., linear programming)

1. Why is the graph of a linear inequality a half plane?

   If you can solve the inequality for y, then it is clear that you are looking for values of y either above $(y > f(x))$ or below $(y < f(x))$ the line. If y doesn't appear in the equation, then the line must be vertical, and the inequality tells you if you are looking for points to the right $(x > a)$ or to the left $(x < a)$ of this line. In the following examples, the boundary lines have been labeled. Dotted boundary lines are not part of the solution set.

   Examples: $y \leq 5, \quad x > -2, \quad x + 2y \geq 3$

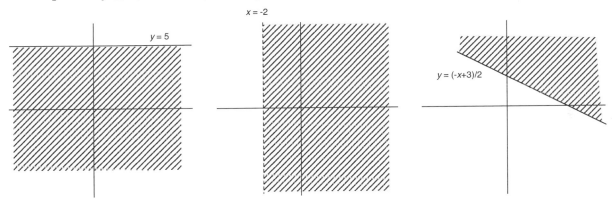

2. How do you apply linear inequalities?

   Linear programming can be used to solve optimization problems in many different fields. Usually, you are asked to maximize some quantity with respect to various linear constraints.

   Simple(x) Example: Say you have 20 days to knit hats and scarves for a friend's store. It takes you 1.5 days to knit a hat and only 1 day to knit a scarf. You plan to charge $20 per hat and $15 per scarf, but your friend says that she wants no more than 16 items from you. How many hats and how many scarves should you knit in order to maximize your revenue?

   ANS: Let x be the number of hats knitted and y the number of scarves knitted. So $x \geq 0$ and $y \geq 0$. Also, $x + y \leq 16$ because your friend only wants 16 items at most. The number of days it takes to knit hats is $1.5x$, while the number of days it takes to knit scarves is y. So $1.5x + y \leq 20$ since there are only 20 days to knit. If we graph all of these inequalities, we obtain a region of all the possible numbers of scarves and hats you could knit. The revenue function is $20x + 15y$, which we would like to maximize on the given region. According to the simplex method, since the revenue condition is linear, we need only check the corners of our region, which occur at any intersection point of two linear conditions.

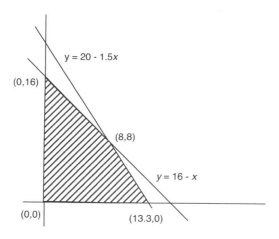

Checking, we get:

- no scarves and no hats yields 0 dollars of revenue
- 16 scarves and no hats yields $(16)(15) = 240$ dollars of revenue
- 8 scarves and 8 hats yields $8(15) + 8(20) = 280$ dollars of revenue
- 13 hats and no scarves yields $13(20) = 260$ dollars of revenue

So, to maximize revenue, you should knit eight scarves and eight hats.

3. Sample Problems

   (a) Sketch the solution to $y \le 2x - 5$.
   (b) Sketch the solution to $2x + 3y > 6$.
   (c) Sketch all the complex numbers $a + bi$ with $a < 2b$.
   (d) Suppose that a company makes two kinds of puzzles: easy and hard. The company has 10 weeks to make puzzles before putting the products on the market. They can make 60 easy puzzles per week and 40 hard puzzles per week. They make \$12 profit on each easy puzzle and \$15 profit on each hard puzzle. Assuming that they can only put 500 puzzles on the market, how many of each should they make?

4. Answers to Sample Problems

   (a) Sketch the solution to $y \le 2x - 5$.

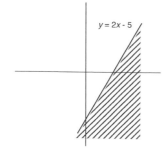

(b) Sketch the solution to $2x + 3y > 6$.

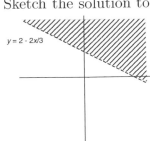

$y = 2 - 2x/3$

(c) Sketch all the complex numbers $a + bi$ with $a < 2b$.

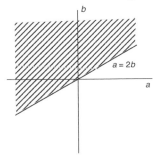

b

$a = 2b$

a

(d) Suppose that a company makes two kinds of puzzles: easy and hard. The company has 10 weeks to make puzzles before putting the products on the market. They can make 60 easy puzzles per week and 40 hard puzzles per week. They make \$12 profit on each easy puzzle and \$15 profit on each hard puzzle. Assuming that they can only put 500 puzzles on the market, how many of each should they make? 300 easy, 200 hard.

The corners of the region of interest are $(0,0)$, $(0,400)$, $(500,0)$, and $(300,200)$, where x is the number of easy puzzles made and y is the number of hard puzzles made. Checking each one, we obtain the maximum revenue at $(300,200)$.

b. Prove and use: the Rational Root Theorem for polynomials with integer coefficients; the Factor Theorem; the Conjugate Roots Theorem for polynomial equations with real coefficients; the Quadratic Formula for real and complex quadratic polynomials; the Binomial Theorem

1. What is the Rational Root Theorem for polynomials with integer coefficients?

   If $f(x) = a_n x^n + a_{n-1} x^{n-1} + \ldots + a_1 x + a_0$, with each a_i an integer, then the Rational Root Theorem says that the only possible rational roots are of the form $\pm \frac{p}{q}$, where p is a divisor of a_0 and q is a divisor of a_n.

   Proof: Suppose $\frac{p}{q}$ is a root of f. Then

   $$0 = f(p/q) = a_n (p/q)^n + a_{n-1}(p/q)^{n-1} + \ldots + a_1(p/q) + a_0.$$

   Multiply by q^n to clear denominators. Then

   $$0 = a_n p^n + a_{n-1} p^{n-1} q + \ldots + a_1 p q^{n-1} + a_0 q^n.$$

   So $-a_0 q^n = a_n p^n + a_{n-1} p^{n-1} q + \ldots + a_1 p q^{n-1} = p(a_n p^{n-1} + a_{n-1} p^{n-2} q + \ldots + a_1 q^{n-1})$, which is clearly divisible by p. If we assume that $\frac{p}{q}$ is in lowest terms, then p has no factors in common with q^n. So p must be a divisor of a_0. Similarly, $-a_n p^n = q(a_{n-1}p^{n-1} + \ldots + a_1 pq^{n-2} + a_0 q^{n-1})$, which is divisible by q. Thus, a_n must be divisible by q.   □

Alternate Explanation: Factor $f(x)$ into factors with integer coefficients. If $\pm \frac{p}{q}$ is a root, then $(qx \mp p)$ is a factor. [See Factor Theorem, below.] So, when you multiply out all the factors, q will be a factor of the leading coefficient, a_n, and p will be a factor of the constant term, a_0. [To check this, try multiplying $(2x - 3)$ by any polynomial with integer coefficients. Then notice that the leading term is divisible by 2 and the constant term is divisible by 3.]

Example: List all possible rational roots of $g(x) = 2x^3 + 9x^2 + 7x - 6$.

ANS: Any rational root must be a factor of 6 divided by a factor of 2. The possibilities are: $\pm 1, \pm 2, \pm 3, \pm 6, \pm \frac{1}{2}, \pm \frac{3}{2}$.

2. What is the Factor Theorem?

The Factor Theorem says that $(x - b)$ is a factor of $f(x)$ if and only if $f(b) = 0$.

Proof: The Factor Theorem is just a special case of the Remainder Theorem, which says that if $f(x)$ is divided by $(x - b)$, then the remainder is $f(b)$. To see this, recall that if you divide $f(x)$ by $(x - b)$, you get a quotient polynomial $q(x)$ and a remainder polynomial $r(x)$ with the degree of $r(x)$ smaller than the degree of $(x - b)$. So $r(x)$ must be a constant, say r. Hence we have

$$f(x) = (x - b)q(x) + r.$$

Letting $x = b$ gives the Remainder Theorem: $f(b) = r$. Therefore, $f(b) = 0$ if and only if the remainder is zero, i.e., exactly when $(x - b)$ is a factor of $f(x)$.   □

Example: Find the roots of $f(x) = x^5 + 8x^4 + 19x^3 + 8x^2 - 20x - 16$.

ANS: Using the Remainder Theorem (and synthetic substitution), we notice that both 1 and -1 are roots, which shortens the calculations:

x	1	8	19	8	-20	-16	
1	1	9	28	36	16	0	root
-1	1	8	20	16	0		root
-1	1	7	13	3			(not a double root)
-2	1	6	8	0			root
-2	1	4	0				double root
-4	1	0					root

(You can also try plugging in $1, -1, -2$, and -4 into the polynomial to obtain zero. Review synthetic substitution if you wish to use it.) The roots are : $1, -1, -2$, and -4, where -2 is a double root. This also means that

$$f(x) = x^5 + 8x^4 + 19x^3 + 8x^2 - 20x - 16 = (x - 1)(x + 1)(x + 2)^2(x + 4).$$

3. What is the Conjugate Roots Theorem for polynomial equations with real coefficients?

If $f(x)$ is a polynomial with *real* coefficients, and if $f(a + bi) = 0$, then the Conjugate Roots Theorem says that $f(a - bi) = 0$.

Proof: Since $f(x)$ has real coefficients, $f(x) = \overline{f}(x)$, where $\overline{f}(x)$ is the polynomial obtained by taking the complex conjugate of every coefficient of f. So

$$0 = f(a + bi) = \overline{f(a + bi)} = \overline{f}(\overline{a + bi}) = f(\overline{a + bi}) = f(a - bi). \quad \square$$

Example: Factor $g(x) = x^4 - 5x^3 + 9x^2 - 5x$ if you know that $g(2 + i) = 0$.

ANS: Since $2 + i$ is a root, the Conjugate Roots Theorem says that $2 - i$ is also a root. This means that $(x - (2 + i))$ and $(x - (2 - i))$ are factors of $g(x)$. So

$$
\begin{aligned}
(x - (2 + i))(x - (2 - i)) &= x^2 - (2 + i)x - (2 - i)x + (2 + i)(2 - i) \\
&= x^2 - 4x + 5
\end{aligned}
$$

is also a factor of $g(x)$. Notice that x is a factor as well. So, using long division, (or trial and error, or noticing that 1 is a root), we obtain

$$g(x) = x^4 - 5x^3 + 9x^2 - 5x = x(x - 1)(x^2 - 4x + 5).$$

4. What is the Conjugate Roots Theorem for polynomial equations with rational coefficients? [**not specifically listed on CSET]

   If $f(x)$ is a polynomial with *rational* coefficients, and if $f(a + b\sqrt{n}) = 0$ (with $\sqrt{n}$ irrational), then the Conjugate Roots Theorem says that $f(a - b\sqrt{n}) = 0$.

   Proof: Abstract Algebra. Since f has rational coefficients, f doesn't change when you switch the irrational $\sqrt{n}$ with $-\sqrt{n}$. The proof then is similar to the one using complex conjugation, given above.

   Example: Suppose $f(x)$ is quadratic with $f(5 - \sqrt{5}) = 0$. Find a possible formula for $f(x)$.

   ANS: Let's find such an f with rational coefficients, which means that we can require $f(5 + \sqrt{5}) = 0$ also. The simplest quadratic is thus

$$
\begin{aligned}
f(x) &= (x - (5 - \sqrt{5}))(x - (5 + \sqrt{5})) \\
&= x^2 - (5 - \sqrt{5})x - (5 + \sqrt{5})x + (5 - \sqrt{5})(5 + \sqrt{5}) \\
&= x^2 - 10x + 20.
\end{aligned}
$$

5. What is the Quadratic Formula for real and complex quadratic polynomials?

   If $ax^2 + bx + c = 0$ with $a \neq 0$, then $x = \dfrac{-b \pm \sqrt{b^2 - 4ac}}{2a}$.

   A Cubic Formula and a Quartic Formula also exist, but no Quintic Formula!

6. What is the Binomial Theorem?

$$(x + y)^n = \sum_{k=0}^{n} \binom{n}{k} x^{n-k} y^k,$$

where $\begin{pmatrix} n \\ k \end{pmatrix} = \dfrac{n!}{k!(n-k)!}$ and is read "n choose k." It is also the number of ways to choose k objects from a set of n objects.

The Binomial Theorem can be proved by mathematical induction.

Proof: We start by checking that the formula is true for $n = 1$.

$$\sum_{k=0}^{1} \begin{pmatrix} 1 \\ k \end{pmatrix} x^{1-k} y^k = \begin{pmatrix} 1 \\ 0 \end{pmatrix} x^1 y^0 + \begin{pmatrix} 1 \\ 1 \end{pmatrix} x^0 y^1 = 1x + 1y = (x+y)^1.$$

Now we show that whenever the formula is true for some value of n then it is also true for $n + 1$. (Via induction, this will imply that the formula is true for any value of n.)

$$\begin{aligned}
(x+y)^{n+1} &= (x+y)(x+y)^n \\
&= (x+y)\left(\sum_{k=0}^{n} \begin{pmatrix} n \\ k \end{pmatrix} x^{n-k} y^k \right) \\
&= \sum_{k=0}^{n} \begin{pmatrix} n \\ k \end{pmatrix} x^{n-k+1} y^k + \sum_{k=0}^{n} \begin{pmatrix} n \\ k \end{pmatrix} x^{n-k} y^{k+1}
\end{aligned}$$

We need to re-index the second summation in order to combine like terms correctly. Let $\ell = k + 1$ so that the summation is from $\ell = 1$ to $\ell = n + 1$. Then

$$(x+y)^{n+1} = \sum_{k=0}^{n} \begin{pmatrix} n \\ k \end{pmatrix} x^{n-k+1} y^k + \sum_{\ell=1}^{n+1} \begin{pmatrix} n \\ \ell - 1 \end{pmatrix} x^{n-(\ell-1)} y^{\ell}$$

Notice that we can combine the middle terms ($1 \le k, \ell \le n$) and notice that we have like terms now, if we match up k in the first sum with ℓ in the second, but that the first and last terms need to be separated out.

$$\begin{aligned}
(x+y)^{n+1} &= x^{n+1} + \left(\sum_{k=1}^{n} \left[\begin{pmatrix} n \\ k \end{pmatrix} + \begin{pmatrix} n \\ k-1 \end{pmatrix} \right] x^{n-k+1} y^k \right) + y^{n+1} \\
&= \sum_{k=0}^{n+1} \begin{pmatrix} n+1 \\ k \end{pmatrix} x^{n+1-k} y^k,
\end{aligned}$$

which is exactly what we wanted to show. $\square$

Example: Expand $(x+2)^5$.

$$\begin{aligned}
(x+2)^5 &= \sum_{k=0}^{5} \begin{pmatrix} 5 \\ k \end{pmatrix} x^{5-k} 2^k \\
&= \begin{pmatrix} 5 \\ 0 \end{pmatrix} x^5 2^0 + \begin{pmatrix} 5 \\ 1 \end{pmatrix} x^4 2^1 + \ldots + \begin{pmatrix} 5 \\ 5 \end{pmatrix} x^0 2^5 \\
&= x^5 + 5x^4(2) + 10x^3(4) + 10x^2(8) + 5x(16) + 1(32) \\
&= x^5 + 10x^4 + 40x^3 + 80x^2 + 80x + 32.
\end{aligned}$$

7. Sample Problems

   (a) Show that in $x^2 + bx + c = 0$, the sum of the two roots is $-b$ and the product of the two roots is c.

   (b) Solve $z^2 - iz + 2 = 0$.

   (c) Let $2x^4 - x^3 - 20x^2 + 13x + 30 = 0$.

      i. List all possible rational roots.

      ii. Find all rational roots.

      iii. Find all roots.

   (d) Let $6x^4 + 7x^3 + 6x^2 - 1 = 0$.

      i. List all possible rational roots.

      ii. Find all rational roots.

      iii. Find all roots.

   (e) Factor $x^3 - x - 6$ if you know that one root is $-1 + i\sqrt{2}$.

   (f) Let $f(x) = x^2 - bx + (b - 1)$. Find $f(1)$. Explain how the Factor Theorem allows you to factor $f(x)$. Then, factor $f(x)$.

   (g) Solve $x^2 + 3x = -5$.

   (h) Find the coefficient of x^4 in $(x - 3)^6$.

   (i) Find the fifth term in the expansion of $(2x - y)^9$.

   (j) Derive the Quadratic Formula. [Hint: Complete the Square.]

   (k) Explain why the number of ways to choose k objects from a group of n is the same as the number of ways to choose $n - k$ objects from a group of n.

8. Answers to Sample Problems

   (a) Show that in $x^2 + bx + c = 0$, the sum of the two roots is $-b$ and the product of the two roots is c. The roots are $x = \frac{-b \pm \sqrt{b^2 - 4c}}{2}$. So,

   $$\frac{-b + \sqrt{b^2 - 4c}}{2} + \frac{-b - \sqrt{b^2 - 4c}}{2} = \frac{-2b}{2} = -b,$$

   and

   $$\left(\frac{-b + \sqrt{b^2 - 4c}}{2}\right)\left(\frac{-b - \sqrt{b^2 - 4c}}{2}\right) = \frac{(-b + \sqrt{b^2 - 4c})(-b - \sqrt{b^2 - 4c})}{4}$$

   $$= \frac{(-b)^2 - (b^2 - 4c)}{4} = \frac{4c}{4} = c.$$

   (b) Solve $z^2 - iz + 2 = 0$. Using the Quadratic Formula, we get

   $$z = \frac{i \pm \sqrt{-1 - 4(2)}}{2} = \frac{i \pm \sqrt{-9}}{2} = \frac{i \pm 3i}{2} = 2i, -i.$$

(c) Let $2x^4 - x^3 - 20x^2 + 13x + 30 = 0$.

    i. List all possible rational roots. $\pm 1, \pm 2, \pm 3, \pm 5, \pm 6, \pm 10, \pm 15, \pm 30, \pm \frac{1}{2}, \pm \frac{3}{2}, \pm \frac{5}{2}, \pm \frac{15}{2}$.

    ii. Find all rational roots.

$$2x^4 - x^3 - 20x^2 + 13x + 30 = (x+1)(2x^3 - 3x^2 - 17x + 30) = (x+1)(x-2)(x+3)(2x-5)$$

    So, the rational roots are $-1, 2, -3, \frac{5}{2}$.

    iii. Find all roots. $-1, 2, -3, \frac{5}{2}$. We know the list is complete because the polynomial has degree 4.

(d) Let $6x^4 + 7x^3 + 6x^2 - 1 = 0$.

    i. List all possible rational roots. $\pm 1, \pm \frac{1}{2}, \pm \frac{1}{3}, \pm \frac{1}{6}$.

    ii. Find all rational roots.

$$6x^4 + 7x^3 + 6x^2 - 1 = (2x+1)(3x-1)(x^2 + x + 1)$$

    So, the rational roots are $-\frac{1}{2}$ and $\frac{1}{3}$.

    iii. Find all roots. $-\frac{1}{2}, \frac{1}{3}, \frac{-1 \pm i\sqrt{3}}{2}$.

(e) Factor $x^3 - x - 6$ if you know that one root is $-1 + i\sqrt{2}$. Since the coefficients are real, we know that another root is $-1 - i\sqrt{2}$. Hence

$$(x - (-1 + i\sqrt{2}))(x - (-1 - i\sqrt{2})) = (x + 1 - i\sqrt{2})(x + 1 + i\sqrt{2}) = (x+1)^2 + 2 = x^2 + 2x + 3$$

is a factor of $x^3 - x - 6$. So $x^3 - x - 6 = (x^2 + 2x + 3)(x - 2)$ by long division, or by guess and check, or by looking at the leading coefficient and constant term and deducing the linear factor.

(f) Let $f(x) = x^2 - bx + (b - 1)$. Find $f(1)$. Explain how the Factor Theorem allows you to factor $f(x)$. Then, factor $f(x)$.

$f(1) = 1 - b + (b - 1) = 0$. The Factor Theorem implies that $(x - 1)$ is thus a factor of $f(x)$. So

$$x^2 - bx + (b - 1) = (x - 1)(x - (b - 1)).$$

(g) Solve $x^2 + 3x = -5$. First, we set $x^2 + 3x + 5 = 0$ and use the Quadratic Formula.

$$x = \frac{-3 \pm \sqrt{9 - 4(5)}}{2} = \frac{-3 \pm \sqrt{-11}}{2} = \frac{-3 \pm i\sqrt{11}}{2}.$$

(h) Find the coefficient of x^4 in $(x - 3)^6$. 135. The $k = 2$ term is:

$$\binom{6}{2} x^{6-2}(-3)^2 = 15x^4(9) = 135x^4.$$

(i) Find the fifth term in the expansion of $(2x - y)^9$. The first term corresponds to $k = 0$ in the summation. So the fifth term corresponds to $k = 4$.

$$\binom{9}{4}(2x)^5(-y)^4 = \frac{(9)(8)(7)(6)(5!)}{(4)(3)(2)(1)(5!)}(32x^5)(y^4) = 4032x^5y^4.$$

(j) Derive the Quadratic Formula. [Hint: Complete the Square.]

$$ax^2 + bx + c = 0 \qquad \text{Given } (a \neq 0)$$

$$x^2 + \frac{b}{a}x = -\frac{c}{a} \qquad \text{Divide by } a \neq 0 \text{ and rearrange terms}$$

$$x^2 + \frac{b}{a}x + \frac{b^2}{4a^2} = -\frac{c}{a} + \frac{b^2}{4a^2} \qquad \text{Complete the square}$$

$$\left(x + \frac{b}{2a}\right)^2 = \frac{b^2 - 4ac}{4a^2} \qquad \text{Factor, obtain common denominator}$$

$$\left(x + \frac{b}{2a}\right) = \pm\frac{\sqrt{b^2 - 4ac}}{2a} \qquad \text{Take square root of each side}$$

$$x = -\frac{b}{2a} \pm \frac{\sqrt{b^2 - 4ac}}{2a} \qquad \text{Rearrange terms}$$

and thus $x = \dfrac{-b \pm \sqrt{b^2 - 4ac}}{2a}$.

(k) Explain why the number of ways to choose k objects from a group of n is the same as the number of ways to choose $n - k$ objects from a group of n. If you choose k objects to include in your subgroup, then you could also think of that as simultaneously choosing $n - k$ objects to exclude from your subgroup. Each way to choose a few is also a way to exclude all the rest. Mathematically, this means $\begin{pmatrix} n \\ k \end{pmatrix} = \begin{pmatrix} n \\ n - k \end{pmatrix}$.

c. Analyze and solve polynomial equations with real coefficients using the Fundamental Theorem of Algebra

1. What is the Fundamental Theorem of Algebra?

   The Fundamental Theorem of Algebra says that if $f(x)$ is a polynomial with real coefficients, then $f(x)$ can be factored into linear and quadratic factors, each of which has real coefficients. Moreover, $f(x)$ can be factored entirely into linear factors if you allow your factors to have complex coefficients.

2. How do you use the Fundamental Theorem of Algebra to analyze polynomial equations?

   The main way to use the Fundamental Theorem of Algebra is when determining the number of roots a polynomial has. For example, a polynomial of degree n has at most n roots. Combined with the previous theorems, we can often say more.

   Example: Say f has real coefficients and degree 5. If $2 - i$ is a root of f, then how many real roots can f have? The answer is that f has either one or three real roots. The reason for this is that because f has real coefficients, the Conjugate Roots Theorem says that $2 + i$ is also a root. This accounts for 2 of the roots of f, leaving 3 more complex roots, some of which might (also) be real. Since the complex nonreal roots have to come in conjugate pairs, there are either zero or two more complex nonreal roots. Hence the number of real roots must be three or one. (This includes the multiplicity of a double or triple root, which would count as two or three roots, respectively.)

3. Sample Problems

    (a) Suppose $f(x)$ is a quartic polynomial with integer coefficients. If $f(1 + i) = 0$ and $f(2 - \sqrt{3}) = 0$, then find a possible formula for $f(x)$.

    (b) How many real roots can $x^5 - 3x^2 + x + 1$ have? Be specific.

    (c) Find a possible formula for a polynomial $f(x)$ that satisfies: $f(-2) = f(3) = f(5) = 0$ and $f(0) = 15$.

    (d) If $x^2 - 5x + 6$ is a divisor of the polynomial $f(x)$, then what is the minimum degree of f? What is $f(2)$? What is $f(3)$? Suppose $f(4) = 0$. Find a formula for $f(x)$.

4. Answers to Sample Problems

    (a) Suppose $f(x)$ is a quartic polynomial with integer coefficients. If $f(1 + i) = 0$ and $f(2 - \sqrt{3}) = 0$, then find a possible formula for $f(x)$. Since f has rational coefficients, we can employ both forms of the Conjugate Roots Theorem, implying that f has four roots. One possible formula for f is thus:

$$f(x) = (x - (1 + i))(x - (1 - i))(x - (2 - \sqrt{3}))(x - (2 + \sqrt{3})),$$

    which equals $(x^2 - 2x + 2)(x^2 - 4x + 1) = x^4 - 6x^3 + 11x^2 - 10x + 2$.

    (b) How many real roots can $x^5 - 3x^2 + x + 1$ have? Be specific. This polynomial could have 1, 3, or 5 real roots. However, we can use synthetic substitution (or long division) to see that 1 is a double root. Thus the polynomial must have 3 or 5 real roots.

    (c) Find a possible formula for a polynomial $f(x)$ that satisfies: $f(-2) = f(3) = f(5) = 0$ and $f(0) = 15$. We know that f must have factors $(x + 2)$, $(x - 3)$, and $(x - 5)$. So we could guess $f(x) = (x + 2)(x - 3)(x - 5)$, but this satisfies $f(0) = 30$, which is not what we want. So, we could multiply our guess by $\frac{1}{2}$, which doesn't change the roots. Thus a correct answer is

$$f(x) = \frac{1}{2}(x + 2)(x - 3)(x - 5) = \frac{1}{2}(x^3 - 6x^2 - x + 30) = \frac{1}{2}x^3 - 3x^2 - \frac{1}{2}x + 15.$$

    (d) If $x^2 - 5x + 6$ is a divisor of the polynomial $f(x)$, then what is the minimum degree of f? What is $f(2)$? What is $f(3)$? Suppose $f(4) = 0$. Find a formula for $f(x)$. The minimum degree of f would be 2. Since $2^2 - 5(2) + 6 = 0$, $f(2) = 0$. Similarly, $f(3) = 0$. If we also know that $f(4) = 0$, then f must have a factor of $(x - 4)$ as well, bringing its minimum degree up to 3. One possible formula for $f(x)$ is

$$(x^2 - 5x + 6)(x - 4) = x^3 - 9x^2 + 26x - 24.$$

1.3 Functions

a. Analyze and prove general properties of functions (i.e., domain and range, one-to-one, onto, inverses, composition, and differences between relations and functions)

1. What is a relation?

   A relation from a set A to a set B is a set of ordered pairs (x, y), where $x \in A$ and $y \in B$.

   A relation on the real numbers is a subset of $\mathbb{R} \times \mathbb{R} = \mathbb{R}^2$.

2. What is a function? What are domain and range?

   A function f from A to B is a relation from A to B that satisfies the following two properties:

   (a) for every element $x \in A$, there is an ordered pair $(x, y) \in f$. [We say that $y = f(x)$.]

   (b) if $(x, y) \in f$ and $(x, z) \in f$, then $y = z$.

   One of these properties talks about the *existence* of $f(x)$ and one talks about the *uniqueness* of $f(x)$, both of which are important in the definition of a function. Which is which?

   ANS: The first property establishes the existence of $f(x)$ and the second property establishes its uniqueness.

   The set A is called the *domain* of f.

   The *range* of f is NOT the set B, but rather $\{f(x) : x \in A\} \subseteq B$. The set B is called a *codomain* of f.

   Example: $f : \mathbb{R} \to \mathbb{R}$ given by $f(x) = x^2$. The domain of f is $\mathbb{R}$, but the range of f is ....

   ANS: The range is $[0, \infty)$, the set of non-negative real numbers.

3. What is a one-to-one function?

   A function $f : A \to B$ is one-to-one if, for all $b \in B$, there is at most one $x \subset A$ satisfying $f(x) = b$.

   (a) "Blob" Picture: If f is one-to-one, then each element in the domain maps to a unique element in the range.

   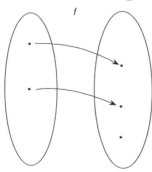

   one-to-one, but not onto

(b) Graphs and horizontal lines: If f is one-to-one, then each horizontal line intersects the graph at most once. (Ex: $f(x) = \sqrt{x}$.)

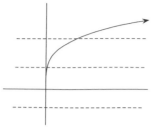

4. What is an onto function?

A function $f : A \rightarrow B$ is onto if, for all $b \in B$, there is at least one $x \in A$ satisfying $f(x) = b$.

(a) "Blob" Picture: If f is onto, then each element in the codomain has at least one element mapping to it.

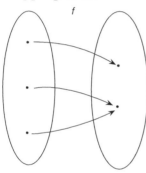

onto, but not one-to-one

(b) Graphs and horizontal lines: If f is onto, then each horizontal line intersects the graph at least once. (Ex: $f(x) = x^3 - x$.)

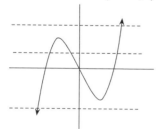

5. Making new functions from old functions

(a) shifts (translations)

To shift the graph of $y = f(x)$ up [resp. down] by k units, you _____ [resp. _____] k to the _____ of the function f. The new graph is $y =$ _____ [resp. _____].

ANS: add, [subtract], output (or y-value), $f(x) + k$, [$f(x) - k$].

To shift the graph of $y = f(x)$ right [resp. left] by k units, you _____ [resp. _____] k to the _____ of the function f. The new graph is $y =$ _____ [resp. _____].

ANS: subtract, [add], input (or x-value), $f(x - k)$, [$f(x + k)$].

(b) stretches and smushes (dilations & compressions)

To stretch the graph of $y = f(x)$ vertically by a factor of d units, you _____ the _____ of the function f by d. The new graph is $y =$ _____.

ANS: multiply, output, $df(x)$.

To stretch the graph of $y = f(x)$ horizontally by a factor of d units, you _____ the _____ of the function f by d. The new graph is $y =$ _____.

ANS: divide, input, $f(\frac{x}{d})$.

(c) reflections

To reflect the graph of $y = f(x)$ over the x-axis, you _____ the _____ of the function f by -1. The new graph is $y =$ _____.

ANS: multiply, output, $-f(x)$.

To reflect the graph of $y = f(x)$ over the y-axis, you _____ the _____ of the function f by -1. The new graph is $y =$ _____.

ANS: multiply (or divide!), input, $f(-x)$.

(d) sum, difference, product, quotient

You can add functions f and g to get a new function: $f + g$. The new function is defined by:

$$(f + g)(x) = f(x) + g(x).$$

The other operations are similar, except that there is one restriction when you divide two functions. What is it?

ANS: You are not allowed to divide by zero. If $g(a) = 0$, then a cannot be in the domain of $(f/g)(x) = \frac{f(x)}{g(x)}$.

(e) composition

In addition to addition, subtraction, multiplication, and division, you can compose two functions to obtain a new one. That is, if $f : A \rightarrow B$ and $g : B \rightarrow C$, then you can compose them to get a new function $h : A \rightarrow C$ defined by $h(x) = g(f(x))$. We say $h = g \circ f$.

Example: $f(x) = x^2$ and $g(x) = x + 3$. Then $(g \circ f)(x) = x^2 + 3$ and $(f \circ g)(x) = (x + 3)^2 = x^2 + 6x + 9$. Notice that $f \circ g$ can be different from $g \circ f$.

(f) inverse functions

Also, if a function $f : A \rightarrow \text{range}(f)$ is one-to-one, then you can define a new function $f^{-1} : \text{range}(f) \rightarrow A$ according to:

$$f^{-1}(b) = x \quad \Longleftrightarrow \quad f(x) = b.$$

The roles of domain and range are swapped.

Example: $f(x) = \dfrac{3x-5}{7}$. Find f^{-1}.

ANS: The usual algorithm involves switching x and y and then solving for y. That is, instead of $y = \frac{3x-5}{7}$, we start with $x = \frac{3y-5}{7}$, which means $7x = 3y - 5$, or $y = \frac{7x+5}{3}$. So $f^{-1}(x) = \dfrac{7x+5}{3}$.

The graph of f^{-1} can be obtained from the graph of f by reflecting over the line $y = x$ (which essentially switches y and x, thus swapping the domain and the range).

(g) identity function $(f(x) = x)$

The identity function is a boring function in one sense, but it plays a necessary role both in inverse functions and in function composition. How so?

ANS: The composition of a function and its inverse should be the identity function (because the inverse function "undoes" whatever the original function does). Also, the composition of any function g with the identity function is equal to the function g. (The identity function is "inert" under composition.)

6. Sample Problems

(a) If $f(x) = 2x^2 - 8$ and if $g(x) = \sqrt{x}$, then what is the domain of $g(f(x))$?

(b) Let $f = \{(1,1),(2,3),(2,4),(3,1)\}$ and let $g = \{(4,3),(3,3),(2,1),(1,4)\}$

   i. Which set is a function?

   ii. What is the domain of that function? ...range ...?

   iii. Is that function one-to-one? Explain.

   iv. Is that function onto the set $\{1,3,4\}$? Explain.

(c) Fill in the table below. If there is not enough information, put a question mark.

x	1	2	3	4	5
$f(x)$	5	4	3	2	1
$g(x)$	3	5	2	1	4
$(f+g)(x)$					
$(g/f)(x)$					
$(g \circ f)(x)$					
$(f \circ g)(x)$					
$g^{-1}(x)$					

(d) If $f(x) = 3x - 5$, then find $f(f(2))$ and $f^{-1}(2)$.

(e) Sketch the graph of $y = f(x) = |x|$ on the domain $[-2, 2]$. Then sketch the following graphs, labeling the vertex and the endpoints.

   i. $y = f(x) - 3$

   ii. $y = f(x - 3)$

   iii. $y = 3f(x)$

    iv. $y = f(3x)$

    v. $y = -f(x)$

    vi. $y = f(-x)$

(f) Find formulas for the following (separate) transformations of $f(x) = x^3 - x$.

    i. Shift f to the right 4 units and then up 2 units.

    ii. Stretch f horizontally by a factor of 5 and then reflect in the y-axis.

    iii. Shift f to the left 3 units, then reflect in the x-axis, and then compress vertically by a factor of 2.

(g) Give an example of functions f and g where $f \neq g$, neither function is the identity, but $f \circ g = g \circ f$.

(h) Find $f^{-1}(x)$ if $f(x) = \frac{5x-2}{3}$. Verify that $f(f^{-1}(x)) = x$ and that $f^{-1}(f(x)) = x$.

7. Answers to Sample Problems

(a) If $f(x) = 2x^2 - 8$ and if $g(x) = \sqrt{x}$, then what is the domain of $g(f(x))$? The set $(-\infty, -2] \cup [2, \infty)$.

(b) Let $f = \{(1,1), (2,3), (2,4), (3,1)\}$ and let $g = \{(4,3), (3,3), (2,1), (1,4)\}$

    i. Which set is a function? g. f is not a function.

    ii. What is the domain of that function? $\{4,3,2,1\}$ range? $\{1,3,4\}$.

    iii. Is that function one-to-one? Explain. NO. $g(4) = g(3) = 3$. Two elements of the domain map to the same element of the range, which means that g is not one-to-one.

    iv. Is that function onto the set $\{1,3,4\}$? Explain. YES. Since g maps to 1, 3, and 4, we say that g is onto the set $\{1,3,4\}$.

(c) Fill in the table below. If there is not enough information, put a question mark.

x	1	2	3	4	5
$f(x)$	5	4	3	2	1
$g(x)$	3	5	2	1	4
$(f+g)(x)$	8	9	5	3	5
$(g/f)(x)$	3/5	5/4	2/3	1/2	4
$(g \circ f)(x)$	4	1	2	5	3
$(f \circ g)(x)$	3	1	4	5	2
$g^{-1}(x)$	4	3	1	5	2

(d) If $f(x) = 3x - 5$, then find $f(f(2))$ and $f^{-1}(2)$. Since $f(2) = 1$, $f(f(2)) = f(1) = -2$. We can find the inverse function directly or use the definition:

$$y = f^{-1}(2) \Leftrightarrow f(y) = 2.$$

So we need to solve $2 = f(y) = 3y - 5$, or $y = f^{-1}(2) = \frac{7}{3}$.

(e) Sketch the graph of $y = f(x) = |x|$ on the domain $[-2, 2]$. Then sketch the following graphs, labeling the vertex and the endpoints. Labels have been left off of the answers, but for the original graph, the vertex is at $(0, 0)$, and the endpoints are $(-2, 2)$ and $(2, 2)$.

    i. $y = f(x) - 3 = |x| - 3$, vertex: $(0, -3)$, endpts: $(-2, -1)$ and $(2, -1)$

    ii. $y = f(x - 3) = |x - 3|$, vertex: $(3, 0)$, endpts: $(1, 2)$ and $(5, 2)$

    iii. $y = 3f(x) = 3|x|$, vertex: $(0, 0)$, endpts: $(-2, 6)$ and $(2, 6)$

    iv. $y = f(3x) = |3x|$, vertex: $(0, 0)$, endpts: $(-\frac{2}{3}, 2)$ and $(\frac{2}{3}, 2)$

    v. $y = -f(x) = -|x|$, vertex: $(0, 0)$, endpts: $(-2, -2)$ and $(2, -2)$

    vi. $y = f(-x) = |-x| = |x|$ (same as original graph)

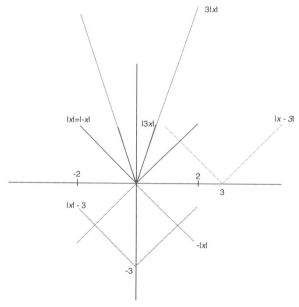

(f) Find formulas for the following (separate) transformations of $f(x) = x^3 - x$.

    i. Shift f to the right 4 units and then up 2 units. $(x - 4)^3 - (x - 4) + 2$

    ii. Stretch f horizontally by a factor of 5 and then reflect in the y-axis. $-(\frac{x}{5})^3 + \frac{x}{5}$

    iii. Shift f to the left 3 units, then reflect in the x-axis, and then compress vertically by a factor of 2. $\frac{1}{2}[(-x + 3)^3 - (-x + 3)]$

(g) Give an example of functions f and g where $f \neq g$, neither function is the identity, but $f \circ g = g \circ f$. There are many answers. For example, $f(x) = x + 3$ and $g(x) = x - 5$. Also, $f(x) = px$ and $g(x) = qx$, where p and q are any real numbers with $p \neq q$.

(h) Find $f^{-1}(x)$ if $f(x) = \frac{5x-2}{3}$. Verify that $f(f^{-1}(x)) = x$ and that $f^{-1}(f(x)) = x$.

$$f^{-1}(x) = \frac{3x+2}{5}.$$

$$f(f^{-1}(x)) = f\left(\frac{3x+2}{5}\right)$$

$$= \frac{5\left(\frac{3x+2}{5}\right) - 2}{3} = \frac{3x+2-2}{3} = x.$$

$$f^{-1}(f(x)) = f^{-1}\left(\frac{5x-2}{3}\right)$$

$$= \frac{3\left(\frac{5x-2}{3}\right) + 2}{5} = \frac{5x-2+2}{5} = x.$$

b. Analyze properties of polynomial, rational, radical, and absolute value functions in a variety of ways (e.g., graphing, solving problems)

1. Continuity and holes

   Polynomials and absolute value functions are continuous on the entire domain of real numbers. Rational functions are continuous everywhere except when the denominator is zero. Radical functions are continuous on their domains, but are not always defined for all reals.

   Examples include: $3x^3 - x$, $|x - 4|$, $\frac{x+3}{x^2-4}$ (discontinuities at $x = \pm 2$), and $\sqrt{x-2}$ (not defined for $x < 2$).

2. Intercepts, horizontal and vertical

   Every function has exactly one vertical intercept, provided that $x = 0$ is in its domain. Functions can have several horizontal intercepts, which can be found by setting the value of the function to zero and solving for x. For example, $x^3 - 2x + 1$ has one vertical intercept at $y = 1$, and three horizontal intercepts. $\frac{-1 \pm \sqrt{5}}{2}$ and 1.

3. Asymptotes, horizontal and vertical

   Polynomials, radicals, and absolute value functions have no asymptotes. Rational functions have horizontal asymptotes exactly when the degree of the numerator is less than or equal to the degree of the denominator. Rational functions can have vertical asymptotes or holes at the points where the denominator is zero. How can you tell which is which? (See example.)

   Example: $f(x) = \frac{x^2 + 4x + 4}{x^2 - 4}$ versus $g(x) = \frac{x^2 + 2x + 1}{x^2 - 4}$

   $f(x)$ can be factored and reduced to $\frac{x+2}{x-2}$, provided that $x \neq -2$. This means that there is a hole in the graph of f at the point $(-2, \frac{-2+2}{-2-2}) = (-2, 0)$. The function $g(x)$ cannot be reduced, which means that the $(x + 2)$ factor cannot be canceled. Thus $g(x)$ has a vertical asymptote at $x = -2$.

4. Sample Problems

(a) Solve for x: $\sqrt{x} + \sqrt{x+3} = 3$.

(b) Find the range of $f(x) = |2x - 5| + 3$ and sketch the graph of $y = f(x)$.

(c) Say that $y = f(x)$ is a cubic polynomial and that $f(3) = f(1) = f(-2) = 0$. Also, say that $f(0) = 12$. Find the formula for f.

(d) What is the [subtle] difference between $f(x) = x + 1$ and $g(x) = \dfrac{x^2 - 1}{x - 1}$? How does this show up on their graphs?

(e) Explain why the domain of $\sqrt{x}$ is $[0, \infty)$ but the domain of $\sqrt[3]{x}$ is all real numbers.

(f) Sketch a graph of $y = \dfrac{x^2 - 1}{x^2 - 4}$, labeling all intercepts and asymptotes.

(g) Sketch a graph of $y = \dfrac{1}{x^2 + 1}$, labeling all intercepts and asymptotes.

(h) Sketch $y = \sqrt{x}$. Then sketch its inverse graph and find the formula. What is the domain of f^{-1} in this case?

(i) Explain why $f(x) = x^2$ is not invertible on its domain of all real numbers, but that it is invertible on the restricted domain $[0, \infty)$.

5. Answers to Sample Problems

(a) Solve for x: $\sqrt{x} + \sqrt{x+3} = 3$. $x = 1$

(b) Find the range of $f(x) = |2x - 5| + 3$ and sketch the graph of $y = f(x)$. The range is $[3, \infty)$.

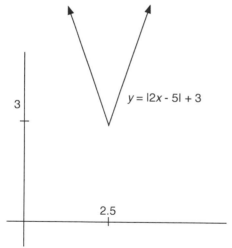

(c) Say that $y = f(x)$ is a cubic polynomial and that $f(3) = f(1) = f(-2) = 0$. Also, say that $f(0) = 12$. Find the formula for f. $f(x) = 2(x-3)(x-1)(x+2) = 2x^3 - 4x^2 - 10x + 12$

(d) What is the [subtle] difference between $f(x) = x + 1$ and $g(x) = \dfrac{x^2 - 1}{x - 1}$? How does this show up on their graphs?

The only difference is that 1 is in the domain of f but it is not in the domain of g. Other than that, the two functions are identical. This means that the graph of $y = g(x)$ is the line $x + 1$ except that it has a hole at the point $(1, 2)$.

(e) Explain why the domain of $\sqrt{x}$ is $[0, \infty)$ but the domain of $\sqrt[3]{x}$ is all real numbers. The square root of a negative number is not real, whereas the cube root of a negative number is negative. For example, since $(-2)^3 = -8$, $\sqrt[3]{-8} = -2$.

(f) Sketch a graph of $y = \dfrac{x^2 - 1}{x^2 - 4}$, labeling all intercepts and asymptotes.

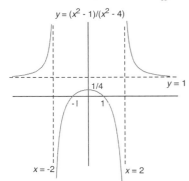

(g) Sketch a graph of $y = \dfrac{1}{x^2 + 1}$, labeling all intercepts and asymptotes.

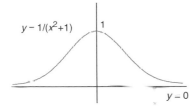

(h) Sketch $y = \sqrt{x}$. Then sketch its inverse graph and find the formula. What is the domain of f^{-1} in this case? The domain of the inverse function is $[0, \infty)$.

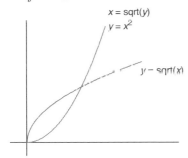

(i) Explain why $f(x) = x^2$ is not invertible on its domain of all real numbers, but that it is invertible on the restricted domain $[0, \infty)$. The function $f(x) = x^2$ is not one-to-one on its domain, $((-2)^2 = 2^2 = 4$, for instance), but it *is* one-to-one on its restricted domain. That means that f is invertible if we only consider non-negative values of x.

c. Analyze properties of exponential and logarithmic functions in a variety of ways (e.g., graphing, solving problems)

*** *For a quick review of logarithms, see the Miscellaneous Topics at the end of this book.*

1. How are exponential and logarithmic functions related?

The exponential and logarithmic functions are inverse functions of each other. So,

- $y = e^x \Leftrightarrow x = \ln y$,
- $y = 10^x \Leftrightarrow x = \log y$, and in general,
- $y = b^x \Leftrightarrow x = \log_b y$.

2. Continuity

   The basic exponential functions are continuous on the entire domain of real numbers.

   The basic logarithmic functions are continuous on their domains (positive real numbers).

3. Intercepts, horizontal and vertical

   The basic exponential functions have only one intercept, at $(0, 1)$.

   The basic logarithmic functions have only one intercept, at $(1, 0)$.

4. Asymptotes, horizontal and vertical

   Exponential functions have one horizontal asymptote, at $y = 0$. As an example, $\lim\limits_{x \to -\infty} 2^x = 0$.

   Logarithmic functions have one vertical asymptote, at $x = 0$. For example, as $x \to 0^+$, $\ln x \to -\infty$.

5. Sample Problems

   (a) Explain the domains and ranges, intercepts, and asymptotes of basic exponential and logarithmic functions in terms of inverse functions.

   (b) Simplify, if possible:

       i. $e^{\ln 4}$

       ii. $\ln(e^{3x})$

       iii. $\log 200 + \log 50$

       iv. $\log_3(2) - \log_3(18)$

       v. $\log_b 1$

       vi. $\log_b 0$

       vii. $10^{\log x + \log x^2}$

   (c) Solve for x: $3 - \log x = 10$.

   (d) Solve for x: $\ln 2^x = \ln 3$.

   (e) Suppose that the value of your \$20,000 car depreciates by 10% each year after you bought it. Find a formula for the value of your car V as a function of t, the number of years since you bought it.

   (f) Suppose that you have money in a bank account earning 5% interest. Then the amount of money you have after t years is given by $A(t) = P(1.05)^t$. where P is the principal amount invested. Find the doubling time of this account. Leave logarithms in your answer.

   (g) Find a formula for an exponential function that passes through the point $(0, 4)$ and the point $(1, 8)$.

(h) Sketch a rough graph of $y = 5 - e^{-x}$. [Hint: Use transformations of a basic graph.] Name a real-world process you could model with a graph of this shape.

6. Answers to Sample Problems

(a) Explain the domains and ranges, intercepts, and asymptotes of basic exponential and logarithmic functions in terms of inverse functions.

Feature	Exponential	Logarithmic
Domain	all reals	$x \geq 0$
Range	$y \geq 0$	all reals
Intercepts	$y = 1$	$x = 1$
Asymptotes	$y = 0$	$x = 0$

Notice that switching x and y (reflecting over the line $y = x$) takes the domain of one function to the range of the other and vice versa. Also, the $y = 1$ intercept of a basic exponential function switches with the $x = 1$ intercept of a basic logarithmic function. Similarly, the horizontal asymptote of a basic exponential function switches with the vertical asymptote of a basic logarithmic function.

(b) Simplify, if possible:

  i. $e^{\ln 4} = 4$

  ii. $\ln(e^{3x}) = 3x$

  iii. $\log 200 + \log 50 = \log 10,000 = 4$

  iv. $\log_3(2) - \log_3(18) = \log_3 \frac{1}{9} = -2$

  v. $\log_b 1 = 0$

  vi. $\log_b 0$ is not defined.

  vii. $10^{\log x + \log x^2} = 10^{\log x^3} = x^3$

(c) Solve for x: $3 - \log x = 10$. $x = 10^{-7}$

(d) Solve for x: $\ln 2^x = \ln 3$. $2^x = 3$; $x - \log_2 3 = \frac{\ln 3}{\ln 2} = \frac{\log 3}{\log 2}$

(e) Suppose that the value of your $20,000 car depreciates by 10% each year after you bought it. Find a formula for the value of your car V as a function of t, the number of years since you bought it. $V(t) = 20,000(0.9)^t$

(f) Suppose that you have money in a bank account earning 5% interest. Then the amount of money you have after t years is given by $A(t) = P(1.05)^t$. where P is the principal amount invested. Find the doubling time of this account. Leave logarithms in your answer.

If $2P = P(1.05)^t$, then $2 = (1.05)^t$, or $t = \log_{1.05} 2 = \frac{\ln 2}{\ln 1.05} = \frac{\log 2}{\log 1.05}$.

(g) Find a formula for an exponential function that passes through the point $(0, 4)$ and the point $(1, 8)$. $y = 4 \cdot 2^x$

(h) Sketch a rough graph of $y = 5 - e^{-x}$. [Hint: Use transformations of a basic graph.] Name a real-world process you could model with a graph of this shape.

Using transformations: you can start with $y = e^x$, flip it over the y-axis to get $y = e^{-x}$, then flip it over the x-axis to get $y = -e^{-x}$. Finally, shift it up five units.

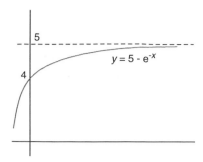

One possible process is heating an object. As the object sits in an oven (at a constant temperature), the object's temperature exponentially approaches the temperature of the oven. There are other valid answers.

1.4 Linear Algebra

a. Understand and apply the geometric interpretation and basic operations of vectors in two and three dimensions, including their scalar multiples and scalar (dot) and cross products

1. What is a vector?

   A vector is a mathematical object that has a magnitude and a direction. People often think of two-dimensional (2-D) vectors as arrows drawn on the plane, and three-dimensional (3-D) vectors as arrows in space. The starting point of a vector is not important to the definition. Consequently, vectors are often depicted in *standard position* (starting at the origin). The magnitude (or length) of $\vec{v}$ is often denoted $\|\vec{v}\|$.

2. What is a vector space?

   A vector space is a set (made up of elements called vectors) that is closed under an operation called vector addition (which is commutative and associative and has an identity and inverses) and under multiplication by a field of scalars (usually the real numbers) which has nice associative and distributive properties over vector addition. The main examples of vector spaces for us will be $\mathbb{R}^2$ (the Cartesian coordinate plane) and $\mathbb{R}^3$ (three-dimensional space).

3. How do you write vectors?

   There are three common main ways to write vectors:

   (a) as ordered n-tuples: $\langle 1, -2 \rangle$ or $\langle -3, 0, 4 \rangle$, [or sometimes as $(1, -2)$ or $(-3, 0, 4)$]

   (b) in terms of component vectors: $\vec{i} - 2\vec{j}$ or $-3\vec{i} + 4\vec{k}$, or

   (c) as columns: $\begin{bmatrix} 1 \\ -2 \end{bmatrix}$ or $\begin{bmatrix} -3 \\ 0 \\ 4 \end{bmatrix}$.

4. How do you add vectors? How do you multiply vectors by scalars?

   Algebraically, you can add vectors by adding their corresponding components. You can multiply a vector by a scalar by multiplying each of its components by that scalar. For example, if $\vec{v} = \langle 1, 4, -6 \rangle$ and $\vec{w} = \langle -3, 0, -2 \rangle$, then:

   $\vec{v} + \vec{w} = \langle 1 + (-3), 4 + 0, (-6) + (-2) \rangle = \langle -2, 4, -8 \rangle$,

   $2\vec{v} = \langle 2(1), 2(4), 2(-6) \rangle = \langle 2, 8, -12 \rangle$,

   and $\vec{v} - \vec{w} = \langle 1 - (-3), 4 - 0, (-6) - (-2) \rangle = \langle 4, 4, -4 \rangle$.

   Geometrically, you can add vectors by drawing one vector at the head of another. You can also multiply a vector by a scalar by scaling the vector by that amount. For example,

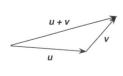

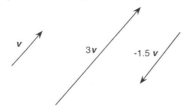

5. How do you "multiply" two vectors?

In general, you cannot multiply vectors, which is one of the ways that they are different from numbers. However, there are two specific products that are useful.

(a) Dot Product (scalar)

The dot product is defined for vectors in any dimension. The dot product of two vectors is always a scalar (and is never a vector). So it's also called the scalar product.

i. Algebraic
If $\vec{v} = \langle v_1, v_2, \ldots, v_n \rangle$ and $\vec{w} = \langle w_1, w_2, \ldots, w_n \rangle$, then

$$\vec{v} \cdot \vec{w} = v_1 w_1 + v_2 w_2 + \ldots + v_n w_n.$$

ii. Geometric
The dot product of two vectors is the product of their lengths times the cosine of the angle between them. That is,

$$\vec{v} \cdot \vec{w} = \|\vec{v}\| \|\vec{w}\| \cos \theta.$$

iii. Why is the dot product important?
The dot product is the easiest way to determine the angle between two vectors. So, it can be used to tell when two vectors are perpendicular. Also, the dot product of a vector with itself gives you the square of the length because $\theta = 0$ in this case. Physicists use the dot product to decompose a vector into its various components. For example, work is the dot product of the force vector with the displacement vector. Force that is perpendicular to the direction of motion ($\theta = 90°$) does not do any work.

(b) Cross Product (vector)

The cross product is only defined for three-dimensional vectors. The cross product of two vectors is always a vector (and is never a scalar). So it's also called the vector product.

i. Algebraic
If $\vec{v} = \langle v_1, v_2, v_3 \rangle$ and $\vec{w} = \langle w_1, w_2, w_3 \rangle$, then

$$\vec{v} \times \vec{w} = \langle v_2 w_3 - v_3 w_2, v_3 w_1 - v_1 w_3, v_1 w_2 - v_2 w_1 \rangle.$$

ii. Geometric
The cross product of two vectors is a vector whose length is the product of the two vectors' lengths times the sine of the angle between them. That is,

$$\|\vec{v} \times \vec{w}\| = \|\vec{v}\| \|\vec{w}\| \sin \theta.$$

Also, the direction of the cross product is perpendicular to the two vectors and points in a direction determined by the Right Hand Rule. Using your right hand, point your fingers in the direction of $\vec{v}$. Keeping your fingers pointing that way, rotate your hand until curling your fingers would make them point in the direction of $\vec{w}$. Now your thumb points in the direction of $\vec{v} \times \vec{w}$.

iii. Why is the cross product important?

The cross product provides a vector that is perpendicular to the plane spanned by two given vectors. Physicists use the cross product with vector quantities and vector fields. For example, torque is the cross product of a force vector with a displacement vector on which the force acts. If a force pulls directly away from a point, ($\theta = 0°$) then that point experiences zero torque from that force.

6. Sample Problems

(a) Draw a picture describing $\langle -3, 5 \rangle + \langle 3, -3 \rangle$.

(b) Draw a picture describing $3 \langle -1, 2 \rangle$.

(c) If $\vec{v}$ has magnitude 13 and points in a direction 135° counter-clockwise from the positive x-axis, then find the magnitude and direction of $2\vec{v}$ and $-3\vec{v}$.

(d) Find the magnitude and direction of $\vec{i} + \vec{j}$.

(e) Give an example showing that the two definitions of the dot product are the same.

(f) Give an example showing that the two definitions of the cross product are the same.

(g) (CSET Sample Test #11) Given any two unit vectors $\vec{a}$ and $\vec{b}$, explain why

$$-1 \le (\vec{a} \cdot \vec{b}) \le 1.$$

(h) Show on a graph that any vector $\vec{v} = v_1 \vec{i} + v_2 \vec{j}$ which is perpendicular to $2\vec{i} + \vec{j}$ has to satisfy $2v_1 + v_2 = 0$. [Hint: think of slopes.]

7. Answers to Sample Problems

(a) Draw a picture describing $\langle -3, 5 \rangle + \langle 3, -3 \rangle$.

(b) Draw a picture describing $3 \langle -1, 2 \rangle$.

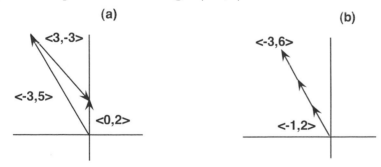

(c) If $\vec{v}$ has magnitude 13 and points in a direction 135° counter-clockwise from the positive x-axis, then find the magnitude and direction of $2\vec{v}$ and $-3\vec{v}$. $2\vec{v}$ has magnitude 26 and points 135° counter-clockwise from the positive x-axis, while $-3\vec{v}$ has magnitude 39, but points 315° counter-clockwise (or 45° clockwise) from the positive x-axis.

(d) Find the magnitude and direction of $\vec{i} + \vec{j}$. The magnitude is $\sqrt{2}$ and the direction is 45° counterclockwise from the positive x-axis.

(e) Give an example showing that the two definitions of the dot product are the same. There are many answers. Consider the example $\langle -1, 1 \rangle \cdot \langle 2, 0 \rangle$. Algebraically, the dot product is $(-1)(2) + (1)(0) = -2$. Geometrically, the magnitude of the first vector is $\sqrt{2}$ and the magnitude of the second vector is 2. The angle between them is $135°$. So the geometric version of the dot product is

$$(\sqrt{2})(2)(\cos 135°) = 2\sqrt{2}\left(-\frac{\sqrt{2}}{2}\right) = -2.$$

(f) Give an example showing that the two definitions of the cross product are the same. There are many answers. Consider the example $\langle 1, 1, 0 \rangle \times \langle 1, 0, 0 \rangle$. There is a $45°$ angle between these vectors. Algebraically, the cross product is $0\vec{i} + 0\vec{j} + (-1)\vec{k} = -\vec{k}$. Geometrically, the magnitude of the cross product is $(\sqrt{2})(1)(\sin 45°) = \sqrt{2}(\frac{\sqrt{2}}{2}) = 1$ and the direction is perpendicular to the xy-plane, in a direction given by the Right Hand Rule. Thus the geometric version of the cross product gives $-\vec{k}$ as well.

(g) (CSET Sample Test #11) Given any two unit vectors $\vec{a}$ and $\vec{b}$, explain why

$$-1 \leq (\vec{a} \cdot \vec{b}) \leq 1.$$

From the geometric version of the dot product, we know that

$$\vec{a} \cdot \vec{b} = \|\vec{a}\|\|\vec{b}\| \cos\theta,$$

where θ is the angle between $\vec{a}$ and $\vec{b}$. Since $\vec{a}$ and $\vec{b}$ are unit vectors, their magnitudes equal 1. So $\vec{a} \cdot \vec{b} = \cos\theta$, which is always between -1 and 1.

(h) Show on a graph that any vector $\vec{v} = v_1\vec{i} + v_2\vec{j}$ which is perpendicular to $2\vec{i} + \vec{j}$ has to satisfy $2v_1 + v_2 = 0$. [Hint: think of slopes.]

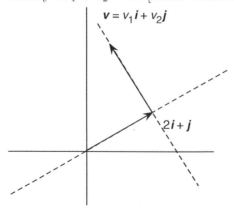

Notice that the slope of any vector $a\vec{i} + b\vec{j}$ is $\frac{\text{rise}}{\text{run}} = \frac{b}{a}$. So the slope of $2\vec{i} + \vec{j}$ is $\frac{1}{2}$. Since perpendicular lines have negative reciprocal slopes, the slope of $\vec{v}$ must be -2. So

$$-2 = \frac{v_2}{v_1} \Rightarrow -2v_1 = v_2 \Rightarrow 0 = 2v_1 + v_2.$$

b. Prove the basic properties of vectors (e.g., perpendicular vectors have zero dot product)

1. What are some basic properties of vectors?

    (a) Assume $\vec{v} \neq \vec{0} \neq \vec{w}$. Then $\vec{v} \cdot \vec{w} = 0$ if and only if $\vec{v} \perp \vec{w}$.
    Proof: From the geometric definition of the dot product (above),

    $$\vec{v} \cdot \vec{w} = \|\vec{v}\|\|\vec{w}\| \cos\theta,$$

    where θ is the angle between $\vec{v}$ and $\vec{w}$. Since the vectors have nonzero lengths, this dot product equals zero if and only if $\cos\theta = 0$. But this means $\theta = 90°$; that is, $\vec{v} \perp \vec{w}$.

    (b) Assume $\vec{v} \neq \vec{0} \neq \vec{w}$. Then $\vec{v} \times \vec{w} = \vec{0}$ if and only if $\vec{v}$ and $\vec{w}$ are parallel or anti-parallel.
    Proof: From the geometric definition of the cross product (above),

    $$\|\vec{v} \times \vec{w}\| = \|\vec{v}\|\|\vec{w}\| \sin\theta,$$

    where θ is the angle between $\vec{v}$ and $\vec{w}$. Since the vectors have nonzero lengths, this dot product equals zero if and only if $\sin\theta = 0$. But this means that either $\theta = 0°$, in which case $\vec{v}$ is parallel to $\vec{w}$, or that $\theta = 180°$, in which case $\vec{v}$ is anti-parallel to $\vec{w}$.

2. Sample Problems

    (a) Let $\vec{v} = 2\vec{i} - 3\vec{j}$ and let $\vec{w} = 7\vec{i} + \vec{j} - 3\vec{k}$. Find the following.

        i. $\vec{v} \cdot \vec{w}$
        ii. $\vec{v} \times \vec{w}$
        iii. $\|\vec{v}\|$ and $\|\vec{w}\|$
        iv. the angle between $\vec{v}$ and $\vec{w}$

    (b) Using the example above, show that $\vec{v} \times \vec{w}$ is perpendicular to $\vec{v}$ and to $\vec{w}$.

    (c) Show that $\vec{v} \times \vec{w}$ is always perpendicular to $\vec{v}$ and to $\vec{w}$.

    (d) Show that $(\vec{v} \times \vec{w}) = -(\vec{w} \times \vec{v})$.

    (e) Show that $\vec{u} \cdot (\vec{v} + \vec{w}) = \vec{u} \cdot \vec{v} + \vec{u} \cdot \vec{w}$. You can assume $\vec{u}$, $\vec{v}$, and $\vec{w}$ are two-dimensional. [The property is true in general.]

    (f) Show that $(\alpha\vec{v}) \cdot \vec{w} = \vec{v} \cdot (\alpha\vec{w}) = \alpha(\vec{v} \cdot \vec{w})$, where α is a scalar (real number). You can assume $\vec{v}$ and $\vec{w}$ are two-dimensional. [The property is true in general.]

    (g) Using the Law of Cosines [In $\triangle ABC$, $c^2 = a^2 + b^2 - 2ab\cos C$.], derive the geometric definition of the dot product. [Hint: draw a triangle of sides $\vec{v}$, $\vec{w}$, and $\vec{w} - \vec{v}$ and apply the formula for length: $\vec{v} \cdot \vec{v} = \|\vec{v}\|^2$.]

3. Answers to Sample Problems

    (a) Let $\vec{v} = 2\vec{i} - 3\vec{j}$ and let $\vec{w} = 7\vec{i} + \vec{j} - 3\vec{k}$. Find the following.

        i. $\vec{v} \cdot \vec{w} = 11$
        ii. $\vec{v} \times \vec{w} = 9\vec{i} + 6\vec{j} + 23\vec{k}$

iii. $\|\vec{v}\| = \sqrt{13}$ and $\|\vec{w}\| = \sqrt{59}$

iv. the angle between $\vec{v}$ and $\vec{w}$ is arccos $\left(\dfrac{11}{\sqrt{767}}\right) \approx 1.16$ radians, or $66.6°$.

(b) Using the example above, show that $\vec{v} \times \vec{w}$ is perpendicular to $\vec{v}$ and to $\vec{w}$. Using the dot product, $\vec{v} \cdot (\vec{v} \times \vec{w}) = 2(9) + (-3)(6) = 18 - 18 = 0$. Similarly, $\vec{w} \cdot (\vec{v} \times \vec{w}) = 7(9) + 1(6) - 3(23) = 63 + 6 - 69 = 0$.

(c) Show that $\vec{v} \times \vec{w}$ is always perpendicular to $\vec{v}$ and to $\vec{w}$. We will show one directly and leave the other part to the reader.

$$
\begin{aligned}
\vec{v} \cdot (\vec{v} \times \vec{w}) &= \langle v_1, v_2, v_3 \rangle \cdot \langle v_2 w_3 - v_3 w_2, v_3 w_1 - v_1 w_3, v_1 w_2 - v_2 w_1 \rangle \\
&= v_1(v_2 w_3 - v_3 w_2) + v_2(v_3 w_1 - v_1 w_3) + v_3(v_1 w_2 - v_2 w_1) \\
&= v_1 v_2 w_3 - v_1 v_3 w_2 + v_2 v_3 w_1 - v_1 v_2 w_3 + v_1 v_3 w_2 - v_2 v_3 w_1 \\
&= 0 + 0 + 0 = 0.
\end{aligned}
$$

Hence, $\vec{v}$ is perpendicular to $\vec{v} \times \vec{w}$. The proof that $\vec{w}$ is perpendicular to $\vec{v} \times \vec{w}$ is similar.

(d) Show that $(\vec{v} \times \vec{w}) = -(\vec{w} \times \vec{v})$.

$$
\begin{aligned}
\vec{v} \times \vec{w} &= \langle v_2 w_3 - v_3 w_2, v_3 w_1 - v_1 w_3, v_1 w_2 - v_2 w_1 \rangle \\
&= \langle -(w_2 v_3 - w_3 v_2), -(w_3 v_1 - w_1 v_3), -(w_1 v_2 - w_2 v_1) \rangle \\
&= -\langle w_2 v_3 - w_3 v_2, w_3 v_1 - w_1 v_3, w_1 v_2 - w_2 v_1 \rangle = -(\vec{w} \times \vec{v}).
\end{aligned}
$$

(e) Show that $\vec{u} \cdot (\vec{v} + \vec{w}) = \vec{u} \cdot \vec{v} + \vec{u} \cdot \vec{w}$. You can assume $\vec{u}$, $\vec{v}$, and $\vec{w}$ are two-dimensional. [The property is true in general.]

Let $\vec{u} = \langle u_1, u_2 \rangle$, $\vec{v} = \langle v_1, v_2 \rangle$, and $\vec{w} = \langle w_1, w_2 \rangle$. Then $\vec{v} + \vec{w} = \langle v_1 + w_1, v_2 + w_2 \rangle$. So,

$$
\begin{aligned}
\vec{u} \cdot (\vec{v} + \vec{w}) &= u_1(v_1 + w_1) + u_2(v_2 + w_2) \\
&= u_1 v_1 + u_1 w_1 + u_2 v_2 + u_2 w_2 \\
&= (u_1 v_1 + u_2 v_2) + (u_1 w_1 + u_2 w_2) \\
&= \vec{u} \cdot \vec{v} + \vec{u} \cdot \vec{w}.
\end{aligned}
$$

(f) Show that $(\alpha \vec{v}) \cdot \vec{w} = \vec{v} \cdot (\alpha \vec{w}) = \alpha(\vec{v} \cdot \vec{w})$, where α is a scalar (real number). You can assume $\vec{v}$ and $\vec{w}$ are two-dimensional. [The property is true in general.]

Let $\vec{v} = \langle v_1, v_2 \rangle$ and $\vec{w} = \langle w_1, w_2 \rangle$. Then $\alpha \vec{v} = \langle \alpha v_1, \alpha v_2 \rangle$.

$$
\begin{aligned}
(\alpha \vec{v}) \cdot \vec{w} &= (\alpha v_1) w_1 + (\alpha v_2) w_2 \\
&= \alpha(v_1 w_1 + v_2 w_2) = \alpha(\vec{v} \cdot \vec{w}) \\
&= v_1(\alpha w_1) + v_2(\alpha w_2) = \vec{v} \cdot (\alpha \vec{w}).
\end{aligned}
$$

(g) Using the Law of Cosines [In $\triangle ABC$, $c^2 = a^2 + b^2 - 2ab\cos C$.], derive the geometric definition of the dot product. [Hint: draw a triangle of sides $\vec{v}$, $\vec{w}$, and $\vec{w} - \vec{v}$ and apply the formula for length: $\vec{v} \cdot \vec{v} = \|\vec{v}\|^2$.]

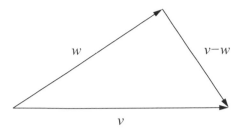

We'll begin with computing the length of the side $\vec{v} - \vec{w}$:

$$
\begin{aligned}
\|\vec{v} - \vec{w}\|^2 &= (\vec{v} - \vec{w}) \cdot (\vec{v} - \vec{w}) \\
&= \vec{v} \cdot \vec{v} - 2\vec{v} \cdot \vec{w} + \vec{w} \cdot \vec{w} \\
&= \|\vec{v}\|^2 + \|\vec{w}\|^2 - 2\vec{v} \cdot \vec{w}.
\end{aligned}
$$

Comparing this to the Law of Cosines, we see that the squares of the side lengths match up, giving $c^2 = a^2 + b^2 - 2\vec{v} \cdot \vec{w}$. Thus

$$
-2ab \cos C = -2\vec{v} \cdot \vec{w},
$$

which means $\vec{v} \cdot \vec{w} = ab \cos C = \|\vec{v}\|\|\vec{w}\| \cos C$, which is what we wanted.   □

c. Understand and apply the basic properties and operations of matrices and determinants (e.g., to determine the solvability of linear systems of equations)

1. What is a matrix?

   A matrix is a rectangular array of numbers. Matrices can be very useful in solving systems of linear equations, among other applications.

2. How do you multiply matrices?

   You can multiply two matrices if the number of columns of the first matrix equals the number of rows of the second matrix. As an example,

   $$
   \begin{bmatrix} a & b \\ c & d \end{bmatrix} \begin{bmatrix} 1 & 2 & 3 \\ 4 & 5 & 6 \end{bmatrix} = \begin{bmatrix} a + 4b & 2a + 5b & 3a + 6b \\ c + 4d & 2c + 5d & 3c + 6d \end{bmatrix}.
   $$

   In general, if A is an m by n matrix and B is an n by p matrix, then AB is an m by p matrix and the entry of AB in row i and column j is given by:

   $$
   (AB)_{ij} = \sum_{k=1}^{n} A_{ik} B_{kj}.
   $$

3. What is the determinant of a matrix?

   The determinant of a square matrix is a specific number that encodes some of the properties of that matrix. For instance, if $\det M = 0$, then the matrix M is not invertible. If $\det M \neq 0$, then there is a matrix N satisfying $MN = NM = I$, where I means the identity matrix (1s on the diagonal, 0s elsewhere). In this case, N is also called M^{-1}, the inverse matrix of M.

For 2 by 2 matrices, the determinant is given by:

$$\det \begin{bmatrix} a & b \\ c & d \end{bmatrix} = \begin{vmatrix} a & b \\ c & d \end{vmatrix} = ad - bc.$$

Also, for 2 by 2 matrices, there is a relatively simple formula for finding the inverse matrix:

$$\begin{bmatrix} a & b \\ c & d \end{bmatrix}^{-1} = \left(\frac{1}{ad - bc} \right) \begin{bmatrix} d & -b \\ -c & a \end{bmatrix}, \text{ if } ad - bc \neq 0.$$

For 3 by 3 matrices, the determinant is given by:

$$\begin{vmatrix} a & b & c \\ d & e & f \\ g & h & i \end{vmatrix} = aei + bfg + cdh - bdi - afh - ceg.$$

One way to remember this formula involves recopying the first two columns and then looking along the diagonals of the resulting array.

$$\begin{array}{ccc|cc} a & b & c & a & b \\ d & e & f & d & e \\ g & h & i & g & h \end{array}$$

Multiplying along diagonals down and to the right, we get the terms aei, bfg, and cdh. These are the first three (positive) terms in the determinant formula. Multiplying down and to the left, we obtain the terms bdi, afh, and ceg, which are the next three (negative) terms in the determinant formula.

There is also a recursive way to find the determinant, called expansion by minors. This means that the determinant of a 3 by 3 matrix (for instance) can be written in terms of determinants of various 2 by 2 submatrices of the original matrix. The tricky part is that there is a factor of $(-1)^{r+c}$, where r is the row number and c the column number, counted from the upper left. We'll expand along the top row, although any row or column would work. Pick the first element, a, and then form a submatrix by deleting the row and column containing a. Continue throughout the row. See the example, below.

$$\begin{aligned}
\begin{vmatrix} a & b & c \\ d & e & f \\ g & h & i \end{vmatrix} &= (-1)^2 a \begin{vmatrix} e & f \\ h & i \end{vmatrix} + (-1)^3 b \begin{vmatrix} d & f \\ g & i \end{vmatrix} + (-1)^4 c \begin{vmatrix} d & e \\ g & h \end{vmatrix} \\
&= a(ei - fh) - b(di - fg) + c(dh - eg) \\
&= aei + bfg + cdh - afh - bdi - ceg.
\end{aligned}$$

Expansion by minors applies to larger matrices, whereas the trick of repeating the first two columns works only for 3 by 3 matrices.

4. How can you use a matrix to determine the solvability of a system of linear equations?

If you have a system of n linear equations in n variables, you can write it as $A\vec{x} = \vec{b}$, where A is the square (n by n) coefficient matrix, $\vec{x}$ is the vector of variables, and $\vec{b}$ is a column vector of right-hand sides to the equations. See Example, below. Method 1 uses row operations, which are really just manipulations of entire equations. For instance, you can multiply an equation by a constant. So, one valid row operation is to multiply the entire row by a constant.

If A is invertible (that is, if $\det A \neq 0$), then there is exactly one solution to the system, namely $\vec{x} = A^{-1}\vec{b}$. Again, see Example, below, Method 2.

If A is not invertible, then the situation is a little trickier. There might be no solutions (in which case the system of equations is *inconsistent*), or there might be an infinite number of solutions. An example of an inconsistent system is $x + y = 1; x + y = 2$. Clearly these two equations cannot simultaneously be true. An example of a system having an infinite number of solutions is $x + y = 1; 2x + 2y = 2$. This system has an entire line of solution points.

5. How can you use a matrix to solve a system of linear equations?

   Example: Solve the equations $2x + 3y = 5$ and $x - y = 5$ simultaneously.

   Method 1 (row operations):

$$\begin{bmatrix} 2 & 3 & 5 \\ 1 & -1 & 5 \end{bmatrix} \sim \begin{bmatrix} 1 & -1 & 5 \\ 2 & 3 & 5 \end{bmatrix} \text{ (switch rows)}$$

$$\sim \begin{bmatrix} 1 & -1 & 5 \\ 0 & 5 & -5 \end{bmatrix} \text{ (add } -2(\text{row 1}) \text{ to row 2)}$$

$$\sim \begin{bmatrix} 1 & -1 & 5 \\ 0 & 1 & -1 \end{bmatrix} \text{ (divide row 2 by 5)}$$

So the equations now read $x - y = 5$ and $y = -1$. We can substitute to find that $x = 4$.

Method 2 (inverse matrices): First, rewrite the system of equations in matrix form:

$$\begin{bmatrix} 2 & 3 \\ 1 & -1 \end{bmatrix} \begin{bmatrix} x \\ y \end{bmatrix} = \begin{bmatrix} 5 \\ 5 \end{bmatrix}.$$

Using the formula for the inverse of a 2 by 2 matrix gives:

$$\begin{bmatrix} 2 & 3 \\ 1 & -1 \end{bmatrix}^{-1} = \left(\frac{1}{(2)(-1) - (3)(1)} \right) \begin{bmatrix} -1 & -3 \\ -1 & 2 \end{bmatrix} = \begin{bmatrix} 1/5 & 3/5 \\ 1/5 & -2/5 \end{bmatrix}.$$

So, we can multiply the original matrix equation on the left to obtain:

$$\begin{bmatrix} 1/5 & 3/5 \\ 1/5 & -2/5 \end{bmatrix} \begin{bmatrix} 2 & 3 \\ 1 & -1 \end{bmatrix} \begin{bmatrix} x \\ y \end{bmatrix} = \begin{bmatrix} 1/5 & 3/5 \\ 1/5 & -2/5 \end{bmatrix} \begin{bmatrix} 5 \\ 5 \end{bmatrix},$$

which simplifies to

$$\begin{bmatrix} 1 & 0 \\ 0 & 1 \end{bmatrix} \begin{bmatrix} x \\ y \end{bmatrix} = \begin{bmatrix} x \\ y \end{bmatrix} = \begin{bmatrix} 4 \\ -1 \end{bmatrix}.$$

Therefore, $(x, y) = (4, -1)$.

6. Sample Problems

   (a) Check the formula for the 2 by 2 inverse matrix by calculating AA^{-1} and $A^{-1}A$.

   (b) Give an example of 2 by 2 matrices A and B satisfying $AB \neq BA$.

   (c) Solve the following system of equations: $4x - 3y = 15$ and $6x + y = 6$.

   (d) Solve the following system of equations: $x - y = 12$ and $-3x + 3y = 3$.

   (e) Describe how to solve the following system and set up the appropriate matrix equation, but do not actually solve the system.

$$\begin{aligned} 34x - 56y + 223z &= 217 \\ 24x + 25y - 100z &= 27 \\ -30x + 29y + 231z &= -429 \end{aligned}$$

   (f) Find the determinant of $\begin{bmatrix} 11 & 6 \\ 2 & -5 \end{bmatrix}$.

   (g) Find the determinant of $\begin{bmatrix} 4 & 3 & 7 \\ 5 & -5 & 4 \\ 0 & -9 & -8 \end{bmatrix}$.

   (h) Find B so that $AB = C$, where $A = \begin{bmatrix} 3 & 5 \\ -3 & 4 \end{bmatrix}$ and $C = \begin{bmatrix} 9 \\ 9 \end{bmatrix}$.

   (i) Using A and C above, find AC, if possible. Then find CA, if possible.

7. Answers to Sample Problems

   (a) Check the formula for the 2 by 2 inverse matrix by calculating AA^{-1} and $A^{-1}A$. We assume $ad - bc \neq 0$ so that the inverse of A is defined.

$$\begin{bmatrix} a & b \\ c & d \end{bmatrix} \left(\frac{1}{ad - bc} \begin{bmatrix} d & -b \\ -c & a \end{bmatrix} \right) = \frac{1}{ad - bc} \begin{bmatrix} ad - bc & -ab + ba \\ cd - dc & -cb + da \end{bmatrix} = \begin{bmatrix} 1 & 0 \\ 0 & 1 \end{bmatrix},$$

$$\left(\frac{1}{ad - bc} \begin{bmatrix} d & -b \\ -c & a \end{bmatrix} \right) \begin{bmatrix} a & b \\ c & d \end{bmatrix} = \frac{1}{ad - bc} \begin{bmatrix} ad - bc & db - bd \\ -ca + ac & -bc + ad \end{bmatrix} = \begin{bmatrix} 1 & 0 \\ 0 & 1 \end{bmatrix}.$$

   (b) Give an example of 2 by 2 matrices A and B satisfying $AB \neq BA$. There are many answers.

$$\begin{bmatrix} 0 & 1 \\ 0 & 0 \end{bmatrix} \begin{bmatrix} 0 & 0 \\ 1 & 0 \end{bmatrix} = \begin{bmatrix} 1 & 0 \\ 0 & 0 \end{bmatrix}, \text{ but } \begin{bmatrix} 0 & 0 \\ 1 & 0 \end{bmatrix} \begin{bmatrix} 0 & 1 \\ 0 & 0 \end{bmatrix} = \begin{bmatrix} 0 & 0 \\ 0 & 1 \end{bmatrix}.$$

   (c) Solve the following system of equations: $4x - 3y = 15$ and $6x + y = 6$.
      Using matrices, we get
$$\begin{bmatrix} 4 & -3 \\ 6 & 1 \end{bmatrix} \begin{bmatrix} x \\ y \end{bmatrix} = \begin{bmatrix} 15 \\ 6 \end{bmatrix}.$$

The inverse of the coefficient matrix is $\dfrac{1}{22}\begin{bmatrix} 1 & 3 \\ -6 & 4 \end{bmatrix}$. So, multiplying both sides (on the left) by this inverse matrix gives:

$$\frac{1}{22}\begin{bmatrix} 1 & 3 \\ -6 & 4 \end{bmatrix}\begin{bmatrix} 4 & -3 \\ 6 & 1 \end{bmatrix}\begin{bmatrix} x \\ y \end{bmatrix} = \frac{1}{22}\begin{bmatrix} 1 & 3 \\ -6 & 4 \end{bmatrix}\begin{bmatrix} 15 \\ 6 \end{bmatrix} = \frac{1}{22}\begin{bmatrix} 33 \\ -66 \end{bmatrix} = \begin{bmatrix} 1.5 \\ -3 \end{bmatrix}.$$

So $x = 1.5$ and $y = -3$.

(d) Solve the following system of equations: $x - y = 12$ and $-3x + 3y = 3$.

Dividing the second equation by -3 gives $x - y = -1$. Hence there are no solutions to this system of equations. The system is inconsistent.

(e) Describe how to solve the following system and set up the appropriate matrix equation, but do not actually solve the system.

$$\begin{aligned} 34x - 56y + 223z &= 217 \\ 24x + 25y - 100z &= 27 \\ -30x + 29y + 231z &= -429 \end{aligned}$$

We can set up a matrix equation and then use row operations or finding an inverse matrix to reduce and solve the system. The corresponding matrix equation is:

$$\begin{bmatrix} 34 & -56 & 223 \\ 24 & 25 & -100 \\ -30 & 29 & 231 \end{bmatrix}\begin{bmatrix} x \\ y \\ z \end{bmatrix} = \begin{bmatrix} 217 \\ 27 \\ -429 \end{bmatrix}.$$

(f) Find the determinant of $\begin{bmatrix} 11 & 6 \\ 2 & -5 \end{bmatrix}$. -67

(g) Find the determinant of $\begin{bmatrix} 4 & 3 & 7 \\ 5 & -5 & 4 \\ 0 & -9 & -8 \end{bmatrix}$. 100

(h) Find B so that $AB = C$, where $A = \begin{bmatrix} 3 & 5 \\ -3 & 4 \end{bmatrix}$ and $C = \begin{bmatrix} 9 \\ 9 \end{bmatrix}$. In order for AB to be a 2 by 1 matrix, we need B to be a 2 by 1 matrix. Let $B = \begin{bmatrix} x \\ y \end{bmatrix}$ and solve. Or, find A^{-1}. Then $B = A^{-1}C$. In any case,

$$B = \begin{bmatrix} -\frac{1}{3} \\ 2 \end{bmatrix}.$$

(i) Using A and C above, find AC, if possible. Then find CA, if possible. $AC = \begin{bmatrix} 72 \\ 9 \end{bmatrix}$. The product CA is not defined because C has only one column, but A has two rows.

3.1 Natural Numbers

a. Prove and use basic properties of natural numbers (e.g., properties of divisibility)

1. What are the natural numbers?

$$\mathbb{N} = \{1, 2, 3, 4, 5, \ldots\}$$

(Often, computer science books include zero in the natural numbers, but most mathematics books do not.) In higher mathematics, the natural numbers are built out of other objects, like sets. Then, the natural numbers are used to define the integers, which are then used to define the rational numbers, which are then used to define the real numbers, which are then used to define the complex numbers.

2. What are some axioms of the natural numbers?

(Remember, axioms do not need to be proved.)

The natural numbers are closed under addition and multiplication, which are commutative and associate operations in which multiplication distributes over addition. Also, the natural numbers are well ordered, which means that if a and b are natural numbers, then either $a \leq b$ or $b \leq a$. It also means that there is a smallest element.

3. What is division in the natural numbers (or integers)?

There is a Division Algorithm in the integers that says the following. If a and b are natural numbers, then there exist *unique* integers q and r (called the *quotient* and *remainder*) satisfying

   (a) $a = qb + r$, and
   (b) $0 \leq r < b$.

Usually, $a \geq b$, although that is not technically necessary. Also, a could be any integer and division would still work.

4. What is divisibility in the natural numbers (or integers)?

Let a and b be natural numbers [respectively, integers], with $b \neq 0$. We say a is **divisible** by b, or b **divides** a, or $b|a$, if there exists a natural number [resp., integer] k satisfying $a = bk$. In other words, the remainder is zero when a is divided by b.

5. What are some properties of divisibility?

Let $a, b, c \in \mathbb{N}$.

   (a) $a|a$.
   (b) If $a|b$ and $b|c$, then $a|c$.
   (c) If $a|b$, then $a|bc$.
   (d) If $c|a$ and $c|b$, then $c|a + b$.

6. Sample Problems

   (a) Let $a, b \in \mathbb{N}$. Prove that the geometric mean of a and b is less than or equal to the arithmetic mean of a and b; that is, $\sqrt{ab} \leq \frac{a+b}{2}$.

   (b) Let $a, b \in \mathbb{N}$. Prove that $\sqrt{ab} = \frac{a+b}{2}$ if and only if $a = b$.

   (c) Prove that a number is divisible by 4 if the number formed by its last two digits is divisible by 4.

   (d) Prove that a number is divisible by 3 if the sum of its digits is divisible by 3. (You may assume the number has three digits, although the property is true in general.)

   (e) Prove that there are an infinite number of Pythagorean triples.

7. Answers to Sample Problems

   (a) Let $a, b \in \mathbb{N}$. Prove that the geometric mean of a and b is less than or equal to the arithmetic mean of a and b; that is, $\sqrt{ab} \leq \frac{a+b}{2}$.

   Since $a - b$ is a real number, $(a - b)^2 \geq 0$. So,

$$
\begin{aligned}
a^2 - 2ab + b^2 &\geq 0 \\
a^2 + 2ab + b^2 &\geq 4ab \\
(a + b)^2 &\geq 4ab \\
a + b &\geq 2\sqrt{ab},
\end{aligned}
$$

where the last step follows because $ab > 0$. Dividing both sides by 2 gives the final result.

   (b) Let $a, b \in \mathbb{N}$. Prove that $\sqrt{ab} = \frac{a+b}{2}$ if and only if $a = b$.

   Multiplying both sides by 2 and then squaring both sides, we get $4ab = a^2 + 2ab + b^2$, or $0 = a^2 - 2ab + b^2 = (a - b)^2$. Thus $a - b$ must equal zero, that is, $a = b$.

   (c) Prove that a number is divisible by 4 if the number formed by its last two digits is divisible by 4.

   Since 100 is divisible by 4, we know that any number times 100 is also divisible by 4. (See properties of divisibility, above.) So we can disregard the digits in the hundreds place and higher, since they will not affect whether the overall number is divisible by 4. Only the tens and ones digits matter. As an example, consider $3424 = 34(100) + 24$. We know that 4 divides 100, and thus $34(100)$ as well. So, 3424 is divisible by 4 if and only if 24 is divisible by 4, which it is. So 3424 is divisible by 4.

   (d) Prove that a number is divisible by 3 if the sum of its digits is divisible by 3. (You may assume the number has three digits, although the property is true in general.)

   Let h, t, and u be the hundreds, tens, and ones digits of the number n. Then

$$n = 100h + 10t + u = (h + t + u) + 99h + 9t.$$

Suppose that the digit sum of n is divisible by 3. Then $h + t + u = 3k$ for some integer k. Then $n = 3k + 99h + 9t = 3(k + 33h + 3t)$. Clearly, n is divisible by 3. As an aside, notice that a similar argument shows that n is divisible by 9 if its digit sum is divisible by 9.

(e) Prove that there are an infinite number of Pythagorean triples.

The easy way to prove this is to prove that $(3, 4, 5)$ is a Pythagorean triple first $[3^2 + 4^2 = 9 + 16 = 25 = 5^2]$. Then we can show that $(3k, 4k, 5k)$ is another Pythagorean triple for any value of k. Indeed,

$$(3k)^2 + (4k)^2 = 9k^2 + 16k^2 = 25k^2 = (5k)^2.$$

So, $(6, 8, 10)$, $(9, 12, 15)$, etc. belong to an infinite chain of Pythagorean triples.

The harder way is to show that there are an infinite number of Pythagorean triples *which are not all multiples of each other.* Let's look at the difference between consecutive squares.

$$(n + 1)^2 - n^2 = n^2 + 2n + 1 - n^2 = 2n + 1$$

This means that every positive odd number, because it can be written as $2n + 1$, is the difference between two consecutive squares. For example, $4^2 - 3^2 = 16 - 9 = 7$. So $7 = 2(3) + 1$ is a difference of two consecutive squares. But 7 is not itself a perfect square, which means we do not get a Pythagorean triple in this case. However, $9 = 2(4) + 1$ is an odd number and a perfect square. In fact, $5^2 - 4^2 = 25 - 16 = 9 = 3^2$, which gives us the Pythagorean triple $(3, 4, 5)$. The next odd square is $25 = 2(12) + 1$. So $13^2 - 12^2 = 169 - 144 = 25 = 5^2$, giving $(5, 12, 13)$ as a Pythagorean triple. The next one in this sequence is $(7, 24, 25)$. Since there are an infinite number of odd perfect squares, we will get an infinite number of Pythagorean triples, no two of which are multiples of each other.

b. Use the Principle of Mathematical Induction to prove results in number theory

1. What is Mathematical Induction?

   If you have a sequence of statements $(S_1, S_2, S_3, \ldots)$ that satisfy the following properties: (1) that S_1 is true, and (2) that if S_k is true, then it follows that S_{k+1} is also true for all $k \in \mathbb{N}$, then the Principle of Mathematical Induction says that every statement in the sequence is true.

2. What is Complete Induction?

   If you have a sequence of statements $(S_1, S_2, S_3, \ldots)$ that satisfy the following properties: (1) that S_1 is true, and (2) that if S_j is true for all $j \leq k$, then it follows that S_{k+1} is also true for all $k \in \mathbb{N}$, then the Principle of Complete Induction says that every statement in the sequence is true.

   The difference here is that in Complete Induction, you are allowed to assume that all the previous statements are true, rather than just the immediate predecessor. This can be very useful if one statement depends on several preceding statements.

3. How does one prove a result by induction?

   To prove a result by induction, one must prove the two parts of the principle. First, one must prove that S_1 is true. Second, one must prove that *if* S_k is true, for some value of k, then S_{k+1} must also be true.

4. Sample Problems (Prove the following statements.)

   (a) $\sum_{i=1}^{n} i = \dfrac{n(n+1)}{2}$ for all $n \in \mathbb{N}$.

   (b) The number $n^3 - n$ is divisible by 6 for any natural number n.

   (c) $13 | (14^n - 1)$ for all $n \in \mathbb{N}$.

   (d) $\sum_{i=1}^{n} i^2 = \dfrac{n(n+1)(2n+1)}{6}$ for all $n \in \mathbb{N}$.

   (e) The sum of the even integers from 2 to $2n$ is $n(n+1)$.

   (f) $\sum_{i=0}^{n} 2^i = 2^{n+1} - 1$ for all $n \in \mathbb{N}$.

5. Answers to Sample Problems

   (a) $\sum_{i=1}^{n} i = \dfrac{n(n+1)}{2}$ for all $n \in \mathbb{N}$.

   Proof: First, we must show that $\sum_{i-1}^{1} i = \dfrac{1(1+1)}{2}$. But $\sum_{i=1}^{1} i = 1 = \dfrac{1(2)}{2}$. So the statement S_1 is true.

   Aside: What is the general statement, S_n?

   ANS: S_n is the statement we are asked to prove at the beginning, namely

   $$\sum_{i=1}^{n} i = \frac{n(n+1)}{2} \text{ for all } n \in \mathbb{N}.$$

   Second, we need to show that if S_k is true for some k, then S_{k+1} is also true. So, we assume that S_k is true for some k. That is, $\sum_{i=1}^{k} i = \dfrac{k(k+1)}{2}$. This will come in handy later. Now we must prove that S_{k+1} is true under this assumption. We will start by looking at the sum of i as i ranges from 1 to $k+1$ and we will algebraically manipulate it to fit the desired formula.

   $$\begin{aligned}
   \sum_{i=1}^{k+1} i &= \left(\sum_{i=1}^{k} i \right) + (k+1) \\
   &= \frac{k(k+1)}{2} + (k+1) \\
   &= (k+1)\left(\frac{k}{2} + 1 \right) \\
   &= \frac{(k+1)(k+2)}{2},
   \end{aligned}$$

which exactly proves that S_{k+1} is true. Therefore, the Principle of Mathematical Induction implies that S_n is true for all n, namely, that $\sum_{i=1}^{n} i = \dfrac{n(n+1)}{2}$. □

(b) The number $n^3 - n$ is divisible by 6 for any natural number n.

Proof: S_1 says that $1^3 - 1$ is divisible by 6. That is true, because $1^3 - 1 = 0 = 6(0)$. Now assume that $k^3 - k$ is divisible by 6, which means that $k^3 - k = 6m$ for some integer m. Consider

$$(k+1)^3 - (k+1) = k^3 + 3k^2 + 3k + 1 - k - 1 = (k^3 - k) + 3k(k+1) = 6m + 3k(k+1),$$

where we used the assumption that $k^3 - k$ is divisible by 6. Notice that for any k, either k or $k+1$ must be even, which means that $3k(k+1)$ is also divisible by 6. Thus, $(k+1)^3 - (k+1)$ is divisible by 6. Therefore, by the Principle of Mathematical Induction, $n^3 - n$ is divisible by 6 for all n. □

(c) $13 \mid (14^n - 1)$ for all $n \in \mathbb{N}$.

Proof: Clearly, $14^1 - 1 = 13$ is divisible by 13. Let's now assume that $14^k - 1$ is divisible by 13. So, $14^k - 1 = 13m$ for some integer m. Then

$$14^{k+1} - 1 = 14(14^k) - 1 = (13+1)(14^k) - 1 = 13(14^k) + (14^k - 1) = 13(14^k) + 13m.$$

Since each term is divisible by 13, then $14^{k+1} - 1$ is also divisible by 13. Therefore, the Principle of Mathematical Induction says that $13 \mid (14^n - 1)$ for all $n \in \mathbb{N}$. □

(d) $\sum_{i=1}^{n} i^2 = \dfrac{n(n+1)(2n+1)}{6}$ for all $n \in \mathbb{N}$.

Proof: When $n = 1$, both sides are equal to 1. So assume that $\sum_{i=1}^{k} i^2 = \dfrac{k(k+1)(2k+1)}{6}$ for some $k \in \mathbb{N}$. Then

$$
\begin{aligned}
\sum_{i=1}^{k+1} i^2 &= \left(\sum_{i=1}^{k} i^2 \right) + (k+1)^2 \\
&= \frac{k(k+1)(2k+1)}{6} + (k+1)^2 \\
&= \left(\frac{k+1}{6} \right) [k(2k+1) + 6(k+1)] \\
&= \left(\frac{k+1}{6} \right) (2k^2 + 7k + 6) \\
&= \frac{(k+1)(k+2)(2k+3)}{6} = \frac{(k+1)((k+1)+1)(2(k+1)+1)}{6},
\end{aligned}
$$

which is exactly the formula we wanted. Therefore, the Principle of Mathematical Induction says that $\sum_{i=1}^{n} i^2 = \dfrac{n(n+1)(2n+1)}{6}$ for all $n \in \mathbb{N}$. □

(e) The sum of the even integers from 2 to $2n$ is $n(n+1)$.

This is the same proof as problem (a), above, except with both sides multiplied by 2.

(f) $\sum_{i=0}^{n} 2^i = 2^{n+1} - 1$ for all $n \in \mathbb{N}$.

Proof: Let $n = 1$. Then $\sum_{i=0}^{1} 2^i = 2^0 + 2^1 = 3 = 2^2 - 1$. So the statement is true when $n = 1$. Assume the statement is true for some $k \in \mathbb{N}$. That means that $\sum_{i=0}^{k} 2^i = 2^{k+1} - 1$.

Then

$$
\begin{aligned}
\sum_{i=0}^{k+1} 2^i &= \left(\sum_{i=0}^{k} 2^i \right) + 2^{k+1} \\
&= (2^{k+1} - 1) + 2^{k+1} \\
&= 2(2^{k+1}) - 1 = 2^{k+2} - 1,
\end{aligned}
$$

which is exactly the formula we wanted. Therefore the Principle of Mathematical Induction says that $\sum_{i=0}^{n} 2^i = 2^{n+1} - 1$ for all $n \in \mathbb{N}$.

c. Know and apply the Euclidean Algorithm

1. What is the Euclidean Algorithm?

   The Euclidean Algorithm is a procedure that returns the greatest common factor (or greatest common divisor, GCD) of two given natural numbers. The input is two natural numbers a and b, with $a \geq b$. The output is the largest natural number which is a factor of both numbers.

2. How does the Euclidean Algorithm work?

   The Euclidean Algorithm (GCD) is a recursive algorithm that can be summarized as follows:

   To find the greatest common factor of a and b (where $a \geq b$), first divide a by b to find q and r satisfying $a = qb + r$ and $0 \leq r < b$. If $r = 0$, then $GCD(a, b) = b$. If $r \neq 0$, then $GCD(a, b) = GCD(b, r)$.

   Example: Find $GCD(15, 6)$.

   ANS: Since $15 = 2(6) + 3$, then $r \neq 0$. So $GCD(15, 6) = GCD(6, 3)$. We repeat the algorithm. Since $6 = 2(3) + 0$, $GCD(6, 3) = 3$. Thus $GCD(15, 6) = 3$.

3. Why does the Euclidean Algorithm work?

   Since $b > r$ at each step, meaning the next remainder $r' < r$, and so on, we have a descending chain of natural numbers: $b, r, r', \ldots$. But in the natural numbers, such a chain has to be finite. There are only a finite number of natural number solutions to $x < b$ for any value of b. Therefore the algorithm will eventually stop.

The algorithm stops at the right answer because the common factors of a and b are exactly the same as the common factors of b and r. This is because $a = qb + r$, and thus $r = a - qb$. If d is a factor of a and b, then d is a factor of $a - qb = r$ as well. Conversely, if d is a factor of b and r, then d is a factor of $qb + r = a$. Since no common factors are gained or lost, the greatest common factor of the original two numbers is preserved through every step of the algorithm.

4. What is an application of Euclidean Algorithm?

   USEFUL FACT: The greatest common factor of a and b is the smallest natural number that can be written as $as + bt$, where s and t are suitably chosen integers. (The integers s and t are not unique, but you can find suitable values via the Euclidean Algorithm.)

5. Sample Problems

   (a) Find the greatest common factor of 123 and 24.

   (b) Find the greatest common factor of 55 and 34.

   (c) Find the greatest common factor of 91 and 35.

   (d) Show that the greatest common factor of $7n + 4$ and $5n + 3$ is 1 for all $n \in \mathbb{N}$.

6. Answers to Sample Problems

   (a) Find the greatest common factor of 123 and 24. 3
       Since $123 = 5(24) + 3$, $GCD(123, 24) = GCD(24, 3)$. Since $24 = 8(3)$, $GCD(24, 3) = 3$.

   (b) Find the greatest common factor of 55 and 34. 1
       $55 = 1(34) + 21; 34 = 1(21) + 13; 21 = 1(13) + 8; 13 = 1(8) + 5; 8 = 1(5) + 3;$
       $5 = 1(3) + 2; 3 = 1(2) + 1; 2 = 2(1) + 0.$

   (c) Find the greatest common factor of 91 and 35. 7
       $91 = 2(35) + 21; 35 = 1(21) + 14; 21 = 1(14) + 7; 14 = 2(7) + 0.$

   (d) Show that the greatest common factor of $7n + 4$ and $5n + 3$ is 1 for all $n \in \mathbb{N}$.
       $7n + 4 = 1(5n + 3) + (2n + 1); 5n + 3 = 2(2n + 1) + n + 1;$
       $2n + 1 = 2(n + 1) - 1; n + 1 = -(n + 1)(-1) + 0.$
       Or, $-5(7n + 4) + 7(5n + 3) = 1$, which means 1 is the greatest common factor. (See USEFUL FACT, above.)

d. Apply the Fundamental Theorem of Arithmetic (e.g., find the greatest common factor and the least common multiple, show that every fraction is equivalent to a unique fraction where the numerator and denominator are relatively prime, prove that the square root of any number, not a perfect square number, is irrational)

1. What is the Fundamental Theorem of Arithmetic?

   The Fundamental Theorem of Arithmetic states that if n is a natural number, then n can be expressed as a product of prime numbers. Moreover, there is only one way to do so, up to a permutation of the prime factors of n. (Here, we allow a "product" to consist of only one prime, or of no primes so that we can say that EVERY natural number, including 1, is a "product" of primes.)

2. What is a prime number?

   The number $n \in \mathbb{N}$ is **prime** if $n > 1$ and the only positive divisors of n are 1 and n. As examples, 7 is prime but 9 is not, because 9 has 3 as a divisor.

3. Why is the Fundamental Theorem of Arithmetic true?

   The first sentence can be proved using Complete Induction. The second sentence can be proved by using the following Helpful Fact.

   Helpful Fact: Let p be a prime. If $p|ab$, then $p|a$ or $p|b$.

   Proof: (of Helpful Fact) Suppose $p|ab$ but p does not divide a. Then the greatest common factor of p and a must be 1, because there are no other factors of p. By the USEFUL FACT, above, there must be integers s and t satisfying $1 = as + pt$. Multiplying both sides by b, we get $b = bas + bpt$. Notice that $p|bas$ (because $p|ab$) and clearly $p|bpt$. Therefore, $p|b$.   □

4. How does one find the greatest common factor and the least common multiple, using the Fundamental Theorem of Arithmetic?

   Here, one can find the unique prime factorization of two numbers and use that information to determine the greatest common factor and the least common multiple. As an example, consider 12 and 18. We know $12 = 2^2 \cdot 3$ and $18 = 2 \cdot 3^2$. Both share a single factor of 2 and a single factor of 3. So, $2 \cdot 3 = 6$ is the greatest common factor. For the least common multiple, notice that we need factors of at least 2^2 and 3^2 in order to have both 12 and 18 as a factor. So, the least common multiple is $2^2 3^2 = 36$.

5. How can fractions be uniquely represented as a ratio of relatively prime integers? (What does relatively prime mean?)

   The numbers a and b are *relatively prime* if they have no common factors. This happens when $GCD(a, b) = 1$. If you are given a fraction, you can use the Fundamental Theorem of Arithmetic to write the numerator and denominator uniquely as products of primes. Then you can cancel any common factors between them. The resulting numerator and denominator will have no common factors, which makes them relatively prime.

6. What are some proofs that $\sqrt{2}$ is irrational?

   *** For a quick review of Proof by Contradiction, see the Miscellaneous Topics at the end of this book.

   (a) Euclid's proof

      (by contradiction) Assume that $\sqrt{2} = \frac{a}{b}$ and that a and b are relatively prime integers. Then $2b^2 = a^2$. Thus a^2 is even, which means that a has to be even. (The square of an odd number is odd.) So, $a = 2c$ for some integer c. Then $2b^2 = 4c^2$, which means $b^2 = 2c^2$. Thus b^2 is even, which means that b has to be even. But this is impossible, because a and b were chosen to be relatively prime; they can't both be even. Therefore, it must be impossible to write $\sqrt{2}$ as $\frac{a}{b}$, which means $\sqrt{2}$ is irrational.

   (b) Another proof

(by contradiction) Assume that $\sqrt{2} = \frac{a}{b}$. Then $2b^2 = a^2$. By the Fundamental Theorem of Arithmetic, the number on the left hand side of this equation must have an odd number of prime factors, and the number on the right hand side must have an even number of prime factors. This is impossible, because there is only one way to write a number (like $2b^2$) as a product of primes. Therefore, it must be impossible to write $\sqrt{2}$ as $\frac{a}{b}$, which means $\sqrt{2}$ is irrational.

7. Sample Problems

   (a) Consider $y = mx + b$, where m and b are rational numbers. Must there be a point on this line that has integer coordinates?

   (b) Consider $y = ax^2 + bx + c$, where a, b, and c are rational numbers. Must there be a point on this parabola that has integer coordinates?

   (c) Prove that $\sqrt{5}$ is irrational.

   (d) Prove or disprove: If x^2 is rational, then x is rational.

   (e) Prove or disprove: If x^2 is irrational, then x is irrational.

   (f) If $n = 2^2 3^3 x^5 y z^2$ and $m = 2^3 3^2 x^3 y^2$, then find the greatest common factor of n and m, and the least common multiple of n and m.

   (g) Show that if (x, y, z) is a Pythagorean triple, and if f is a common factor of x, y, and z, then $(\frac{x}{f}, \frac{y}{f}, \frac{z}{f})$ is also a Pythagorean triple.

   (h) How many natural number solutions are there to $x + y = 12$? ...to $x + y = n \in \mathbb{N}$?

   (i) How many natural number solutions are there to $xy = 12$? ...to $xy = n \in \mathbb{N}$?

8. Answers to Sample Problems

   (a) Consider $y = mx + b$, where m and b are rational numbers. Must there be a point on this line that has integer coordinates?

   Not necessarily. For example, if $y = \frac{1}{3}x + \frac{1}{2}$, no matter what integer you plug in for x, y will not come out to an exact integer.

   (b) Consider $y = ax^2 + bx + c$, where a, b, and c are rational numbers. Must there be a point on this parabola that has integer coordinates?

   Not necessarily. The example given in the previous problem (with $a = 0$) still works. Also, if $a = b = c = \frac{1}{2}$, then for any integer x, y is equal to an integer plus $\frac{1}{2}$.

   (c) Prove that $\sqrt{5}$ is irrational. We can mimic the proof given above that $\sqrt{2}$ is irrational.
   Proof: Assume that $\sqrt{5} = \frac{a}{b}$. Then $5b^2 = a^2$. By the Fundamental Theorem of Arithmetic, the number on the left hand side of this equation must have an odd number of prime factors, and the number on the right hand side must have an even number of prime factors. This is impossible, because there is only one way to write a number (like $5b^2$) as a product of primes. Therefore, it must be impossible to write $\sqrt{5}$ as $\frac{a}{b}$, which means $\sqrt{5}$ is irrational.

(d) Prove or disprove: If x^2 is rational, then x is rational.

FALSE. Suppose $x^2 = 2$, which is rational. Then $x = \pm\sqrt{2}$, which was proven to be irrational. Thus the statement is false.

(e) Prove or disprove: If x^2 is irrational, then x is irrational.

Proof: Assume that x is rational. Then $x = \frac{p}{q}$ for some integers p and q, with $q \neq 0$. Then $x^2 = \frac{p^2}{q^2}$, which is clearly rational. Therefore, by indirect reasoning (contrapositive), we have shown that if x^2 is irrational, then x must be irrational too.

(f) If $n = 2^2 3^3 x^5 y z^2$ and $m = 2^3 3^2 x^3 y^2$, then find the greatest common factor of n and m, and the least common multiple of n and m.

The greatest common factor of n and m is $2^2 3^2 x^3 y$ and their least common multiple is $2^3 3^3 x^5 y^2 z^2$.

(g) Show that if (x, y, z) is a Pythagorean triple, and if f is a common factor of x, y, and z, then $(\frac{x}{f}, \frac{y}{f}, \frac{z}{f})$ is also a Pythagorean triple.

$$\left(\frac{x}{f}\right)^2 + \left(\frac{y}{f}\right)^2 = \frac{x^2 + y^2}{f^2} = \frac{z^2}{f^2} = \left(\frac{z}{f}\right)^2$$

(h) How many natural number solutions are there to $x + y = 12$? ...to $x + y = n \in \mathbb{N}$? For the first equation, x can be any number between 1 and 11. So there are 11 solutions. (Some of these are essentially the same, like $1 + 11$ and $11 + 1$, but we ignore that similarity here because the solutions have distinct x-values.) For the second equation, then, there are $n - 1$ solutions.

(i) How many natural number solutions are there to $xy = 12$? ...to $xy = n \in \mathbb{N}$? For the first equation, there are 6 solutions, one for each factor of 12: $1, 2, 3, 4, 6, 12$. (Again, solutions are different if they have distinct x-values.) For the second equation, the answer is the number of factors of n. If n is prime, for example, then the answer is 2.

Miscellaneous Extra Review Topics

a. Logarithms

1. What is a logarithm?

   A logarithm is an exponent. The logarithm base b of n is the exponent needed on b to obtain n. In symbols:

   $$x = \log_b n \iff b^x = n.$$

   Any simple logarithmic equation can be transformed into an exponential equation according to the formula above. One consequence of this definition is that you cannot take the logarithm of a number unless that number is positive. This is because basic exponential functions only take positive values.

   Example: Find $\log_3 \frac{1}{81}$.

   Let $x = \log_3 \frac{1}{81}$. Then $3^x = \frac{1}{81} = \frac{1}{3^4} = 3^{-4}$. So, $x = -4$. Therefore, $\log_3 \frac{1}{81} = -4$.

2. What are some bases for logarithms?

   The bases most often used are 10 and e. Logs base 10 are called "common" logs and are written "log" (with no subscript). Logs base e are called "natural" logs and are written "ln."

   Aside: By the way, $e \approx 2.718281828459045\ldots$ One reason e is so useful has to do with calculus. The slope of the graph of $y = e^x$ at any point is equal to the y-coordinate of that point. So, e^x is its own derivative. (See Derivatives, Test 3 materials.)

3. What are some properties of logarithms?

   The following properties hold for any base, b.

   (a) $x = \log_b n \iff b^x = n$ (the definition)

   (b) $\log_b(x^m) = m \log_b x$

   (c) $\log_b(xy) = \log_b x + \log_b y$

   (d) $\log_b x = \dfrac{\log x}{\log b} = \dfrac{\ln x}{\ln b} = \dfrac{\log_a x}{\log_a b}$ (for any base a) [Change of Base Formula]

   The following facts may help you solve log problems.

   (a) $\log_b 1 = 0$. (In particular, $\log 1 = \ln 1 = 0$.)

   (b) $\log_b b = 1$. (In particular, $\log 10 = \ln e = 1$.)

   (c) $\log_b 0$ is not defined.

   (d) $b^{\log_b x} = x$. (In particular, $10^{\log x} = e^{\ln x} = x$.)

   More properties can be found in the Sample Problems.

   Example: Simplify $\log 16 + \log 125 - \log 2$.

Answer: Using the properties, we can deduce that $\log_b \frac{x}{y} = \log_b x - \log_b y$. (See Sample Problems, below.) So, working backwards, we get

$$
\begin{aligned}
\log 16 + \log 125 - \log 2 &= \log \frac{(16)(125)}{(2)} \\
&= \log 1000 \\
&= \log 10^3 \\
&= 3 \log 10 \\
&= 3.
\end{aligned}
$$

4. Sample Problems

   (a) Simplify, if possible:

       i. $\log_4 64$

       ii. $\log_2 128$

       iii. $\log 0.000001$

       iv. $\ln e^{-1}$

       v. $\ln(-e)$

       vi. $\log_7 7$

       vii. $e^{\ln 4}$

       viii. $\log_2 5 - \log_2 40$

       ix. $\log_2 4^t$

       x. $e^{2 \ln w}$

       xi. $\log 10^{4x}$

       xii. $(\log e)(\ln 10)$ [Hint: Use the Change of Base Formula.]

   (b) Write as a single logarithm: $2 \ln w + 5 \ln x - \frac{1}{2} \ln y$.

   (c) Expand as a sum of logarithms of single variables: $\log_5 \left(\frac{x^7}{y^2 \sqrt[3]{z}} \right)$.

   (d) Solve for x: $\log_6 x + \log_6(x + 5) = 1$.

   (e) Why does $\log_6 x - \log_6(x + 5) = 1$ not have a real solution?

   (f) Using the log properties, show that $\log_b b^m = m$.

   (g) Using the log properties, show that $\log_b \frac{x}{y} = \log_b x - \log_b y$.

5. Answers to Sample Problems

   (a) Simplify, if possible:

       i. $\log_4 64 = 3$

       ii. $\log_2 128 = 7$

       iii. $\log 0.000001 = -6$

       iv. $\ln e^{-1} = -1$

    v. $\ln(-e)$ is not defined.

    vi. $\log_7 7 = 1$

    vii. $e^{\ln 4} = 4$

    viii. $\log_2 5 - \log_2 40 = \log_2(\frac{1}{8}) = -3$

    ix. $\log_2 4^t = \log_2(2^{2t}) = 2t$

    x. $e^{2\ln w} = e^{\ln w^2} = w^2$

    xi. $\log 10^{4x} = 4x$

    xii. $(\log e)(\ln 10) = \left(\dfrac{\ln e}{\ln 10}\right)(\ln 10) = 1$

(b) Write as a single logarithm: $2\ln w + 5\ln x - \frac{1}{2}\ln y$. $\ln\left(\dfrac{w^2 x^5}{\sqrt{y}}\right)$

(c) Expand as a sum of logarithms of single variables: $\log_5\left(\dfrac{x^7}{y^2 \sqrt[3]{z}}\right)$.

$$7\log_5 x - 2\log_5 y - \frac{1}{3}\log_5 z$$

(d) Solve for x: $\log_6 x + \log_6(x+5) = 1$. $x = 1$ ($x = -6$ is extraneous)

$$\log_6 x + \log_6(x+5) = 1 \Rightarrow \log_6(x(x+5)) = 1 \Rightarrow x(x+5) = 6 \Rightarrow$$

$$\Rightarrow x^2 + 5x - 6 = 0 \Rightarrow (x+6)(x-1) = 0 \Rightarrow x = 1 \text{ or } -6$$

Checking both of these shows that -6 is extraneous.

(e) Why does $\log_6 x - \log_6(x+5) = 1$ not have a real solution? If we proceed as in the previous problem, we get $\frac{x}{x+5} = 6$, which has $x = -6$ as a solution. But since $\log_6(-6)$ is not defined, there is no solution to the original equation.

(f) Using the log properties, show that $\log_b b^m = m$. Answers may vary.

$$\log_b b^m = m(\log_b b) = m(1) = m.$$

(g) Using the log properties, show that $\log_b \frac{x}{y} = \log_b x - \log_b y$. Answers may vary.

$$\log_b \frac{x}{y} = \log_b(xy^{-1}) = \log_b x + \log_b(y^{-1}) = \log_b x - \log_b y.$$

b. Proof by Contradiction

1. What is a proof by contradiction?

A proof by contradiction is a way to show that a statement is true by showing that it cannot be false. You assume that it is false, and then show that your assumption leads to a contradiction of some other mathematical fact or hypothesis of the problem.

Aside: This proof technique relies HEAVILY on the "Law of the Excluded Middle," which says that either a mathematical statement is true or else it is false. There is no room for any other outcome.

2. Sample Problems

   (a) Let m be an integer and let m^2 be odd. Then m is odd.

   (b) Let $r, s \in \mathbb{R}$ and let $r + s$ be irrational. Then r is irrational or s is irrational.

   (c) Let m and n be integers and let mn be odd. Then m is odd and n is odd.

   (d) Suppose that n is an integer which is not divisible by 3. Then n is not divisible by 6.

   (e) Prove that $\log_2 3$ is irrational.

3. Answers to Sample Problems

   (a) Let m be an integer and let m^2 be odd. Then m is odd.

     Proof: Suppose that m^2 is odd, but m is even. Then $m = 2k$ for some integer k. So $m^2 = 4k^2 = 2(2k^2)$, which is also even. But this contradicts our hypothesis that m^2 is odd. Therefore m must be odd. $\quad\square$

   (b) Let $r, s \in \mathbb{R}$ and let $r + s$ be irrational. Then r is irrational or s is irrational.

     Proof: Suppose that $r + s$ is irrational, but both r and s are rational. Then there exist integers a, b, c, and d with $b \neq 0 \neq d$ such that $r = \frac{a}{b}$ and $s = \frac{c}{d}$. Then $r + s = \frac{a}{b} + \frac{c}{d} = \frac{ad+bc}{bd}$, which is clearly rational. But this contradicts our hypothesis that $r + s$ is irrational. Therefore r is irrational or s is irrational. $\quad\square$

   (c) Let m and n be integers and let mn be odd. Then m is odd and n is odd.

     Proof: Suppose that mn is odd, but either m or n is even. Without loss of generality, say $m = 2k$ for some integer k. Then $mn = 2kn$, which is clearly even. But this contradicts our hypothesis that mn is odd. So therefore m and n must be odd. $\quad\square$

   (d) Suppose that n is an integer which is not divisible by 3. Then n is not divisible by 6.

     Proof: Suppose that n is not divisible by 3, but that n is divisible by 6. Then there exists an integer k satisfying $n = 6k = 3(2k)$. Thus n is also divisible by 3. But this contradicts our hypothesis that n is not divisible by 3. Therefore, n must not be divisible by 6. $\quad\square$

   (e) Prove that $\log_2 3$ is irrational.

     Proof: Suppose that $\log_2 3$ is rational. Then $\log_2 3 = \frac{p}{q}$ for some integers p and q with $q \neq 0$. Then $2^{p/q} = 3$, or, raising both sides to the q-th power, $2^p = 3^q$. According to the Fundamental Theorem of Arithmetic, the only power of 2 that is also a power of 3 is the number $1 = 2^0 = 3^0$. So $p = q = 0$. But this contradicts the fact that $q \neq 0$. Therefore, $\log_2 3$ must be irrational. $\quad\square$

Made in the USA
San Bernardino, CA
14 February 2015